AMERICAN
WAR LIBRARY

★ ★ ★ ★

★ The Cold War ★

ESPIONAGE

Titles in the American War Library series include:

The American Revolution
Generals of the Revolutionary War
Life of a Soldier in
  Washington's Army
Patriots of the Revolutionary War
Primary Sources: American
  Revolution
Strategic Battles
Weapons of War

The Civil War
Leaders of the North and South
Life Among the Soldiers and
  Cavalry
Lincoln and the Abolition of
  Slavery
Strategic Battles
Weapons of War

World War I
Flying Aces
Leaders and Generals
Life in the Trenches
Primary Sources: World War I
Strategic Battles
Weapons of War

World War II
Hitler and the Nazis
Kamikazes
Leaders and Generals
Life as a POW
Life of an American Soldier in
  Europe

Primary Sources: World War II
Strategic Battles in Europe
Strategic Battles in the Pacific
The War at Home
Weapons of War

The Cold War
The Battlefront: Other Nations
Containing the Communists:
  America's Foreign Entanglements
The Cold War Ends: 1980 to the
  Present
The Homefront
Political Leaders
Primary Sources: Cold War
An Uneasy Peace: 1945–1980
Weapons of Peace: The Nuclear
  Arms Race

The Vietnam War
History of U.S. Involvement
The Home Front: Americans
  Protest the War
Leaders and Generals
Life as a POW
Life of an American Soldier
Primary Sources: Vietnam War
Weapons of War

The Persian Gulf War
Leaders and Generals
Life of an American Soldier
The War Against Iraq
Weapons of War

★ The Cold War ★

ESPIONAGE

by Jennifer Keeley

LUCENT
BOOKS®

THOMSON
★
™
GALE

San Diego • Detroit • New York • San Francisco • Cleveland • New Haven, Conn. • Waterville, Maine • London • Munich

On cover: Ethel and Julius Rosenberg (second from right), KGB spies during the Cold War

© 2003 by Lucent Books. Lucent Books is an imprint of The Gale Group, Inc., a division of Thomson Learning, Inc.

Lucent Books® and Thomson Learning™ are trademarks used herein under license.

For more information, contact
Lucent Books
27500 Drake Rd.
Farmington Hills, MI 48334-3535
Or you can visit our Internet site at http://www.gale.com

LIBRARY OF CONGRESS CATALOGING-IN-PUBLICATION DATA

Keeley, Jennifer, 1974–
    Espionage / by Jennifer Keeley.
         p. cm. — (American war library. Cold War series)
Includes bibliographical references and index.
Summary: Discusses the agents, communications, technological advances, covert actions, and double agents during the Cold War.
    ISBN 1-59018-210-3 (alk. paper)
    1. Spies—Juvenile literature. 2. Cold War—Juvenile literature. 3. Espionage, American—History—20th century—Juvenile literature. 4. Espionage, Soviet—History—20th century—Juvenile literature. [1. Espionage. 2. Spies. 3. Cold War.] I. Title. II. Series.
    UB270.5 .K44 2003
    327.1273047'09'045—dc21

2002002218

★ Contents ★

Foreword 6

Introduction: The Importance of
   Espionage in the Cold War 8

Chapter 1: Officers and Agents 14

Chapter 2: Cloak-and-Dagger Work in the Cold War . . . 28

Chapter 3: Technology and the
   Changing Role of the Spy 40

Chapter 4: Listening In: Communications
   Intelligence During the Cold War 49

Chapter 5: Active Measures and Covert Operations 60

Chapter 6: The Cold War Heats Up 71

Chapter 7: Counterintelligence 85

Epilogue: The Post–Cold War World 95

Notes. 97

For Further Reading 100

Works Consulted 101

Index 105

Picture Credits. 111

About the Author 112

A Nation Forged by War

The United States, like many nations, was forged and defined by war. Despite Benjamin Franklin's opinion that "There never was a good war or a bad peace," the United States owes its very existence to the War of Independence, one to which Franklin wholeheartedly subscribed. The country forged by war in 1776 was tempered and made stronger by the Civil War in the 1860s.

The Texas Revolution, the Mexican-American War, and the Spanish-American War expanded the country's borders and gave it overseas possessions. These wars made the United States a world power, but this status came with a price, as the nation became a key but reluctant player in both World War I and World War II.

Each successive war further defined the country's role on the world stage. Following World War II, U.S. foreign policy redefined itself to focus on the role of defender, not only of the freedom of its own citizens, but also of the freedom of people everywhere. During the cold war that followed World War II until the collapse of the Soviet Union, defending the world meant fighting communism. This goal, manifested in the Korean and Vietnam conflicts, proved elusive, and soured the American public on its achievability. As the United States emerged as the world's sole superpower, American foreign policy has been guided less by national interest and more on protecting international human rights. But as involvement in Somalia and Kosovo proves, this goal has been equally elusive.

As a result, the country's view of itself changed. Bolstered by victories in World Wars I and II, Americans first relished the role of protector. But, as war followed war in a seemingly endless procession, Americans began to doubt their leaders, their motives, and themselves. The Vietnam War especially caused people to question the validity of sending its young people to die in places where they were not particularly wanted and for people who did not seem especially grateful.

While the most obvious changes brought about by America's wars have been geopolitical in nature, many other aspects of society have been touched. War often does not bring about change directly, but acts instead like the catalyst in a chemical reaction, accelerating changes already in progress.

Some of these changes have been societal. The role of women in the United States had been slowly changing, but World War II put thousands into the workforce and into uniform. They might have gone back to being housewives after the war, but equality, once experienced, would not be forgotten.

Likewise, wars have accelerated technological change. The necessity for faster airplanes and a more destructive bomb led to the development of jet planes and nuclear energy. Artificial fibers developed for parachutes in the 1940s were used in the clothing of the 1950s.

Lucent Books' American War Library covers key wars in the development of the nation. Each war is covered in several volumes, to allow for more detail, context, and to provide volumes on often neglected subjects, such as the kamikazes of World War II, or weapons used in the Civil War. As with all Lucent Books, notes, annotated bibliographies, and appendixes such as glossaries give students a launching point for further research. In addition, sidebars and archival photographs enhance the text. Together, each volume in the American War Library will aid students in understanding how America's wars have shaped and changed its politics, economics, and society.

The Importance of Espionage in the Cold War

The Cold War began as World War II came to an end. After the war, each one of the Big Three (the United States, the Soviet Union, and Great Britain) had different concerns about the structure of the postwar world. Joseph Stalin, the leader of the Soviet Union (Union of Soviet Socialist Republics or USSR), was in search of security for his nation. Germany had attacked the Soviets twice in thirty years, and both times the Germans had reached them through Poland. Therefore, Stalin thought it was necessary to create a buffer zone between Germany and the Soviet Union. Believing his nation would be safe if bordered to the west by states loyal to Moscow (the Soviet capitol), he directed his foreign intelligence agency (later called the KGB) to rig elections and use brute force to ensure the loyalties of the governments of these bordering states (also called "satellite" states because they orbit the western border of Russia).

The U.S. government wanted a number of things in the postwar world: peace, the chance to bring American troops home safe and sound, and trade, among others. As the war drew to a close, the United States had the strongest military and a monopoly on the atomic bomb. However, despite this superiority, the U.S. officials were increasingly troubled by the expansion of the Soviets into Eastern Europe. The American ambassador to Moscow wrote to the White House warning President Roosevelt that "unless we take issue with the present policy [of the Soviets forcibly taking over Eastern Europe], there is every indication that the Soviet Union will become a world bully."[1] The Soviets were equally distrustful of the U.S. government because they knew it had successfully developed an atomic weapon and feared it might be used against them in the event of war.

The resulting situation was one in which two incredibly powerful nations—

the Soviet Union and the United States—became deeply suspicious of each other, each fearing the other was likely to attack. In addition to these fears, the United States and the USSR conflicted because their societies were based on two different political and economic systems. The U.S. political system is often referred to as a democracy (it is actually a democratic republic) because citizens elect people to represent them in their local, state, and federal government. Meanwhile, the United States has a capitalist economic system in which property, goods, and the means of producing them can be privately owned. The Soviet Union, on the other hand, had a Communist economic and political system. Communism refers to the political and economic system based on the theories of Karl Marx and Vladimir Ilyich Lenin in which the laborers rise up and overthrow the capitalist order and then establish a society where all goods and property are communally owned.

Since a central tenet of communism is the overthrowing of capitalism, hostility grew between the capitalist United States and the Communist Soviet Union. This antagonism increased until each country felt threatened by—and at times paranoid about—the other superpower's plans (imagined or real) to destroy their

American troops stand guard near the Berlin Wall in 1961.

Europe During the Cold War

DENMARK
NETHERLANDS
BRITAIN
BELGIUM
LUXEMBOURG
WEST GERMANY
EAST GERMANY
POLAND
USSR
CZECHOSLOVAKIA
SWITZERLAND
AUSTRIA
HUNGARY
FRANCE
ITALY
ROMANIA
YUGOSLAVIA
SPAIN
ALBANIA

Countries under Soviet rule

force committed fanatically to the belief that . . . the internal harmony of [U.S.] society be disrupted, our traditional way of life be destroyed, the international authority of our state be broken, if Soviet power is to be secure.[2]

"way of life." This type of fear was expressed by George F. Kennan, the U.S. ambassador to Moscow, at the end of World War II:

> In foreign countries Communists will . . . work towards destruction of all forms of personal independence—economic, political, or moral. . . . In general, all Soviet efforts . . . will be negative and destructive in character, designed to tear down sources of strength beyond the reach of Soviet control . . . we have here a political

Just as the United States believed its democratic political system, capitalist economy, and general way of life had to be protected from the Soviets, the Soviets believed their political and economic system of communism had to be safeguarded. Each superpower assumed its system was better and would ultimately prevail. Each country was willing to do everything in its power to ensure victory. Therefore, over the course of the next forty-plus years, the fears and suspicions of these two powerful nations and the actions that resulted from them shaped and reshaped the world. This period, in which hostility existed between the United States and the USSR and an intense ideological battle between their respective political and economic systems was fought without ever developing into outright war, is called the Cold War.

The Need to Spy During the Cold War

In the atmosphere of intense distrust that existed between the United States and Soviet Union during the Cold War, each superpower feared the other would mount an attack, nuclear or otherwise. It, therefore, became important to each superpower to make certain it had the military advantage. The key to maintaining this advantage was to have better technology and weapons, which required developing new technologies, knowing about the technologies being developed by the other side, and having a first-rate warning system that would warn of any attack the other superpower might be planning.

Unsurprisingly, neither the United States nor the USSR willingly told the other about the technology and weapons they developed. Also, neither superpower would warn the other should it decide to attack. Access to information such as this was essential, but the only way to get it was to gather it secretly and without the other superpower's knowledge. Each superpower, therefore, spied on the other in an attempt to ascertain its opponent's plans.

The Intelligence Agencies Gather Information

Each country turned to its intelligence community to meet these needs for the

An atomic bomb is detonated by the United States at the Bikini Atoll test site in 1946.

clandestine gathering of information. In the United States there are a number of organizations that deal in the collection and analysis of information about other nations. Some of these focus on military intelligence. The National Security Agency (NSA), the Defense Intelligence Agency (DIA), Army Intelligence, Navy Intelligence, and Air Force Intelligence, for example, all focus on gathering military information about other nations. These agencies, in combination with some smaller intelligence organizations, are all under the jurisdiction of the Central Intelligence Agency (CIA), which was founded in 1947 to act as the top dog of all the intelligence services in the United States and coordinate the intelligence gathered by all of the other civilian and military agencies.

The Soviets, on the other hand, had no need to create a centralized intelli-gence agency in the early years of the Cold War. They already possessed a much older and more advanced intelli-gence agency that continued to evolve and change to meet the challenges of the Cold War. Since the outset of World War II, the Soviet State Security organi-zation has been called the NKVD, the GUGB, the NKGB, the MGB, K1, the MVD, and finally the KGB in 1953. While all these different names and ini-tials suggest that drastic changes oc-curred in the organization, in reality it simply evolved throughout the twentieth century, taking on new names, new du-ties, and reporting to new departments. Therefore, for ease in understanding, the term KGB will be used to discuss the Soviet State Security organization through-

Korean refugees fleeing war cross into South Korea in 1951.

out the Cold War. The KGB is a huge organization that deals with both domestic and foreign intelligence. Within the organization, the collection of intelligence on foreign nations is handled primarily by one department, the First Chief Directorate (FCD).

Other Roles Played by the KGB and the CIA in the Cold War

However, CIA and KGB officers and agents were asked to do more than simply collect highly protected information. Each nation wanted to win the Cold War and thereby prove that their way of life was superior, and both superpowers equated winning with having the most allies throughout the world. Therefore, the United States and the USSR did anything and everything to stop the other from gaining more influence in nations around the world where it was unclear whether their governments would be-

come Communist or democratic. Since no nation likes other governments meddling in its affairs, all of these actions had to be carried out secretly so they could not be traced back to whichever superpower initiated them. The CIA and KGB employees were already trained to be stealthy, sneaky, and cover their tracks, so it was these individuals who were called upon by their respective nations to participate in covert operations designed to influence the foreign governments.

Thus, for more than forty years the United States and USSR battled each other all over the globe collecting each other's secrets, ferreting out each other's spies, and organizing secret operations to influence foreign governments. While the two superpowers' military forces never directly confronted each other, their intelligence agencies waged a fierce battle. In this battle, the spy slowly evolved into a soldier.

Chapter 1

Officers and Agents

Both the CIA and KGB First Chief Directorate employed thousands of officers and agents who performed a number of duties for the agencies. Intent on winning the battle of brains, each agency searched for the best and brightest to have in its service. They employed, recruited, and trained these individuals to secretly gather information around the globe. Whether an individual worked as an officer or an agent, there were certain aspects of his or her job as a Cold War CIA or KGB employee that were markedly different from any other occupation.

Espionage

Espionage, the practice of spying to obtain secret information, took on many forms during the Cold War. One way to get access to another nation's most carefully guarded secrets is to make contact with people who know them and get them to divulge this information. Therefore, throughout the Cold War, the KGB

and the CIA employed officers called case officers whose job was the recruiting of people who knew secrets, called agents. The officer then had to convince the agent to divulge this information. Since the information is collected from human beings, this is called human intelligence, or HUMINT.

When people hear "CIA" or "KGB" they typically think of intelligence officers similar to those depicted in Hollywood movies, like the glamorous James Bond. However, Bond is far from the typical spy. In reality, espionage can—and should—be very ordinary, commonplace, and mundane. If all spies lived like James Bond, they would stick out like sore thumbs. The spy's job is to blend into society, and their stories are rarely told because, as author Harry Rositzke writes,

> Straight narratives of simple spying, fact or fiction, make dull stories. A man copies a document, delivers it to

his handler, and goes home. The same routine repeated time and time again makes up the career of a spy. Good spies are quiet spies. . . . James Bond is not a spy but a noisy adventurer.[3]

There are a great many spies whose lives are nothing like Bond's or other Hollywood spies. Former CIA officer, David W. Doyle, points out that real intelligence officers (he uses the term "agent" to refer to both officers and agents) play a variety of roles:

Agents come in all shapes and sizes, all ages, genders and nationalities. They play one or more of various roles. There are straight espionage agents, who collect and report intelligence information. There are support agents, who help operations by supplying such services as surveillance, safe-house renting and staffing, clearing or filling dead drops . . . and checking for surveillance—maybe from an apartment, or watching to see if your car is followed. . . .

There are penetration agents—now often called 'moles'; covert action agents; double agents and triple agents. There are even piston agents,

Motion picture spy James Bond in the 1999 film The World Is Not Enough. *The life of a real spy is quite different.*

who go back and forth depending on which service pays more—until they're caught at it, which most eventually are. . . . Stay-behind and sleeper agents may wait twenty years or more to be activated. There are agents who believe they are working for a different service or country than is the case, known as false-flag recruitments.[4]

Becoming an Officer

Men and women worked for intelligence organizations for a variety of reasons during the Cold War: Some truly believed in either communism or anticommunism and worked as officers in order to help spread their ideology across the globe. Others were motivated by career goals, money, excitement, or friendship.

Individuals could pursue careers as CIA or KGB officers just as a person would any other job. They could simply put in a job application or express interest in another fashion. However, neither the KGB nor the CIA relied on willing applicants as their only means of hiring officers; both agencies searched far and wide for the best and the brightest individuals to recruit into their service. Top officers were recruited from the ranks of the military. For instance, many Cold War CIA operatives began their careers in World War II as officers in the armed forces, and the KGB frequently recruited from military organizations in the Soviet Union such as its Red Army. Other officers were originally recruited as agents

and then worked their way up in the organization.

Top universities were also fertile ground for recruiting since many bright, talented people attended them. Universities invited foreign students to attend, and both the CIA and the KGB found these individuals to be excellent recruits since they often returned to their countries and assumed positions of power and influence, which gave them access to high-level information. Plus, the agencies could approach these students when they were young, away from home, and, therefore, more easily influenced.

The best officers were typically those motivated, at least in part, by ideology. This was true because an officer whose goal it was to see either communism or capitalism and democracy triumph was less likely to respond to bribes or blackmail from an opposing intelligence agency. Realizing this, the KGB frequently recruited its agents from Communist Party members at universities throughout the world. It was a KGB officer named Arnold Deutch who "invented" this type of recruiting in the early 1930s. It yielded unprecedented results and would be used by the KGB for years to come.

Deutch's idea was to target the Communist groups at some of Great Britain's premier universities where powerful Brits sent their children. Deutch suggested recruiting young, future leaders while they were in school, just before they became people of power. In this manner, he re-

The KGB often recruited students from top universities, such as these Oxford University undergraduates.

cruited twenty-nine people to work for the KGB, and five of them went on to become incredibly powerful British citizens. According to Deutch, part of the beauty of this type of recruiting was that no one would care if they had once been Communist Party members in college. He said,

> Communists [in colleges] whom [the KGB could] pluck out of the Party . . . [could] pass unnoticed, both by the Party itself and by the outside world. People [would] forget about them. And if they [did] remember they were once Communists, this

[would] be put down to a passing fancy of youth.[5]

Establishing Cover

The recruiting of an agent actually begins with the intelligence officer establishing "cover." In his book, *Silent Warfare,* Abram Shulsky explains cover and the reason for it:

> Since they must avoid the attention of the government of the country in which they are posted, intelligence officers cannot simply hang out a shingle advertising their willingness to pay cash for secrets. They require what in intelligence jargon is called "cover," that is, a plausible reason for being in the country, visible means of financial support, a pretext for meeting people with access to sensitive information, and so forth.[6]

While all such officers who work abroad must have cover, a distinction is made based on whether or not they have official or nonofficial cover. Officers with official cover are stationed in embassies abroad as representatives of their country's government, usually posing as diplomats, ambassadors, or other government officials. As a result, the country in which they are stationed knows they are officials of a foreign government; hopefully it is not known that they actually are undercover intelligence officers.

Recruiting Using Blackmail

Blackmail was a technique employed by both agencies to recruit potential agents. In his book, *Inside the KGB: An Expose by an Officer of the Third Directorate*, Aleksei Myagkov describes the recruiting of a woman, whom he calls N, using such methods:

> From 1966 onwards, she had visited relatives on several occasions in Bad Grünwald in the GDR [German Democratic Republic (East Germany)]. The KGB, who as usual were checking the arrival lists of Westerners, took an interest in her. They decided to exploit her for the information she could provide on West Germany. An agent made her acquaintance, as it were, "by chance." He established a very close relationship with romantic overtones, and later introduced her to a "friend," a KGB officer. The "friend" referred to the difficulties of pronouncing her real name and called her Mariya. "Better and simpler," he explained. At one of their meetings, the agent handed over to N an expensive present on behalf of his absent friend and asked her to write a note of thanks to his address. N, quite un-suspectingly, wrote the following note to the "friend:" "Thank you for your valuable present. I am very pleased. Mariya."

> The KGB intended to use this note as a form of blackmail in N's recruitment. Indeed, the contents of the note were very similar to an agent's receipt working under the pseudonym "Mariya" who had just received a reward for a task she had executed. All this provided an opportunity, in the event of N being stubborn, of forcing her to co-operate by threatening to compromise her and to expose her to the West Germans as a KGB agent.

> Several days later the "friend" himself turned up on N's doorstep with a note. N thanked him for the present. Then the "friend" declared himself to be an employee of the KGB and suggested that she should co-operate, promising a good reward. With much hesitation, N replied in the affirmative; a speedy acknowledgement of the efficacy of KGB blackmail and threats.

On the other hand, officers with non-official cover, or NOCs, reside in a foreign country without that government's knowledge of their connection to either the country they come from or the intelligence agency for which they work. NOCs may pose as bona fide citizens of the foreign country—or they may be bona fide citizens. Or they may position themselves as citizens of their own or another country who are living abroad.

Typically, NOCs use a different cover for each agent whom they recruit. For instance, the officer may be posing as a professor at Duke University in North Carolina to recruit a student there and, at the same time, be posing as a bookstore owner in the Dominican Republic to recruit one of its citizens. Since each cover story requires an elaborate façade, and agents run (handled) by the same officer can be located in different countries, one former Defense Intelligence Agency case officer says "it's difficult—nearly impossible—to run more than three agents because you [must] have three separate identities."[7] He added that these fake identities usually have their own story and set of "pocket litter." Pocket litter is all the small touches that make the cover story believable. For instance, an officer posing as a man with a wife and two children would carry pictures of them as part of his pocket litter. If he has more than three sets of pocket litter to keep track of, and his other identities are as a bachelor, the odds of the picture of the wife and children accidentally showing up in the bachelor's wallet are greatly increased.

Recruiting Agents

The actual recruiting of an agent usually begins with a "talent spotter." A talent spotter is an officer whose job it is to look for potential agents—people who either have direct access to protected information or know people who do. A talent spotter's cover can be anything from a university professor to a clergyman, but it is usually some sort of occupation in which he or she interacts

An actor in a 1957 film plays the role of a CO, gathering information about a potential agent.

with numerous people so that it is possible to spot talent.

Once a potential agent is identified by a talent spotter, the case officer (CO), called a "controller" by the Soviets, begins gathering information on the individual and developing a plan that includes the proper cover to use when approaching this person. One former case officer (CO) recalled an instance when it was necessary to get information from a country's Minister of Trade. He decided it was best to approach this diplomat through his nephew because of the young man's close relationship with his uncle. In doing research on the nephew, the CO learned the young man was on the national tennis team and that he enjoyed foods such as shrimp and champagne. He used this information to approach the minister.

It was arranged for the CO to be present at a cocktail party where the nephew was also in attendance. This sort of casual first meeting is frequently used in espionage. Upon meeting the nephew, the CO "came off as arrogant,"[8] pretending to be a phenomenal tennis player. By the end of the evening, the CO and the nephew had arranged to meet and play. Since the CO could not play tennis, he showed up the day of their match carrying champagne and prawns, wearing a cast and pretending he had broken his arm. The two sat, ate prawns, drank champagne, and started a friendship. After meeting a few more times as friends,

the CO was invited to a party at the nephew's home where the uncle was also present. He could now approach the Minister of Trade.

After meeting a potential agent, the CO then decides the best way to persuade him or her to give the information to a foreign intelligence officer. Flattery, bribery, friendship, sex, blackmail, and brute force are just some of the tactics officers consider for use in getting the information they need. After deciding on the best method, the CO then stages an attempt to get the person to work as an agent. This is called a "pitch." Former KGB officer, Aleksei Myagkov (operating under the alias "Andrey"), recalled working with his commanding officer Boychenko to make a pitch to an East German agent, K. First they tried to convince K to willingly work for the KGB. When this did not work, they switched tactics and resorted to blackmail. Boychenko told K:

> We have no desire to speak to you about unpleasant things but you force me to do so. So then, if you refuse to collaborate, we shall act as follows: firstly we shall compromise you . . . [by] persuading certain of your acquaintances that you have been collaborating for a long time with the KGB. If this were to happen, it seems to me that life in Bernau might not be very pleasant for you. Secondly, as I understand it, you possess a private workshop? [K replies "yes"] And that

son of yours is hoping to study in university? [K replies "yes"]

Well then, you know that we are in a position to ruin everything. . . . You will lose your workshop, your son will never study in university. As you see, the future of your family and its welfare lies in your hands.[9]

It is not typically a choice to become an agent when approached by either the KGB or CIA. They usually find a way to get the information they want.

The KGB or CIA can recruit anyone with access to information at anytime. However, the U.S. intelligence community does honor a hands-off list, which singles out groups of people that cannot be approached as agents. It includes, among others, anyone who has ever worked for the Peace Corps, people who have received Fulbright scholarships, and Rhodes scholars. The reasoning behind

CIA Dead Drops

In *The Spy Who Saved the World: How a Soviet Colonel Changed the Course of the Cold War,* authors Jerrold L. Schecter and Peter S. Deriabin include documents that describe the location and the method for using a CIA dead drop:

Address and Location:

Moscow, corner of Proezd Khudozhestvennogo Teatra and Pushkinskaya ulitsa. The dead drop is located in the main entrance (foyer) of Number 2, located on Pushkinskaya ulitsa—between store Number 19 "Myaso" and the store "Zhenskaya obuv."

The main entrance is open 24 hours a day. The entrance is not guarded, there is no elevator.

In the entrance (foyer)—to the left/upon entering therein/a dial telephone, No. 28, is located. Opposite the dial telephone/to the right as one goes into the entrance hall/is a steam heat radiator, painted in oil paint in a dark green color. This radiator is supported by a single metal hook, fastened into the wall./If one stands facing the radi-ator, then the metal hook will be to the right, at the level of one's hand hanging from the arm./

Between the wall, to which the hook is attached, and the radiator there is a space of two-three centimeters.

For the dead drop, it is proposed to use the hook and the space/open space/between the wall and the radiator.

Method of Using the Dead Drop:

It is necessary to place and camouflage any written material, for example, in a match box, then, the box should be wrapped with soft wire/of a green color/, and the end of the wire bent hook-shaped, which will permit the small box to hang from the hook (or bracket) of the radiator between the wall and the radiator.

The location of the dead drop is on the unlighted right-hand corner of the entrance hall. In the entrance hall it is convenient to make a call on the dial telephone and it is very simple and easy to hang some type of small object on the indicated hook.

the hands-off list is simple. If a Peace Corps volunteer were found to be working as an agent of the CIA, it would compromise the Peace Corps. People may jump to the conclusion that numerous Peace Corps volunteers were agents, and foreign leaders may decide not to allow the Peace Corps to operate in their nation.

Training in Tradecraft

New CIA or KGB recruits must then learn how to be spies. All the methods, tricks, and secrets used in espionage that new agents are instructed in are collectively referred to as tradecraft. Agents for both agencies usually are taught only the tradecraft they need to know to do their job effectively, such as how to spot information and relay it back. CIA officers, on the other hand, typically receive extensive instruction in tradecraft. Whenever possible they are trained at "the farm," Camp Peary in southern Virginia, although some are taught at other secure locations. Similarly, KGB officers usually attend a KGB school for instruction.

The instruction that Aleksei Myagkov received in KGB school is a good example of this type of extensive training in tradecraft. Myagkov began his career in the Soviet Red Army. At the age of twenty-two he decided to become an officer in the KGB and attended KGB School 311 in Novosibirsk, Siberia. In his book, *Inside the KGB*, Myagkov recalls the subjects taught at the school. Some of the topics he studied

were general, such as criminal law, KGB history, and scientific communism. However, he was also instructed in a variety of special disciplines—special discipline No. 2: the intelligence and counterintelligence departments of main enemies (the United States), special discipline No. 5: working for the KGB in war, and special discipline No. 6: intelligence activities of the KGB. Special discipline No. 1: the operational activities of KGB departments, was the main subject. According to Myagkov, it included many of the things he had to master in order to work as a spy:

> The task of KGB departments. The agents' branch of departments (i.e. the selection and preparation of individuals for recruitment as agents, training and education of agents, methods of working with them, etc). Conducting various operations (combined operations, "games"). Misinformation. Work against enemy intelligence services. Work against anti-Soviet personalities. Work against the church and sects. Work against the intelligentsia. Countering the "ideological diversions" of the enemy.[10]

Myagkov's account of the topics covered at KGB school offers insight into the training of its officers. It also highlights one of the main differences between the CIA officer and the KGB officer. The KGB not only concerned itself with foreign intelligence, it also acted as a police force within the Soviet Union. In the United States, gathering intelligence about and policing American citizens is left to the Federal Bureau of Investigation (FBI).

In the case of agents, it was essential that the training itself was done secretly and in a secure place. Frequently a safe house—a dwelling not under surveillance by an opposing intelligence organization—in a third country was used for training purposes. Here the new agent

An FBI poster warns Americans to be on the lookout for spies.

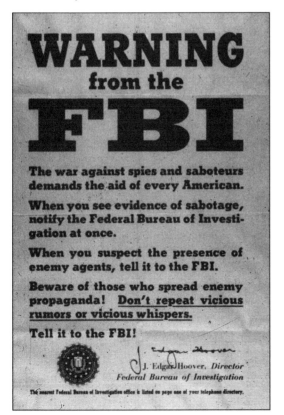

WARNING
from the
FBI

The war against spies and saboteurs demands the aid of every American.

When you see evidence of sabotage, notify the Federal Bureau of Investigation at once.

When you suspect the presence of enemy agents, tell it to the FBI.

Beware of those who spread enemy propaganda! Don't repeat vicious rumors or vicious whispers.

Tell it to the FBI!

J. Edgar Hoover, *Director*
Federal Bureau of Investigation

learned how to go about getting the necessary information without arousing suspicion and how to pass it on to his or her case officer/controller.

A new agent or officer may learn any number of tradecraft secrets. In his book, *The Night Watch,* David Atlee Phillips describes some of the tradecraft he learned in his initial training to be a CIA officer:

> I learned that, when I told a case officer on the telephone I would meet him at the Roxy Theater at eleven, I really meant under the clock at the Biltmore at twelve. . . . I learned recognition procedures: "You go into the men's room at the movie with a copy of *Newsweek* in your left hand. You say to the agent, 'Haven't we met in Cairo?' If he answers 'No, but I seem to remember you from Alexandria,' the meeting is okay." [The training agent] taught me how to make a "brush pass," when a case officer ostensibly bumps into his agent accidentally but when they part there has been a quick exchange of documents, perhaps folded in identical newspapers. I practiced loading "dead drops," public receptacles where papers or packages can be stashed and picked up later without any personal meeting.[11]

When being trained for Cold War operations, officers and agents also learned how to tell if they are being followed or watched by a hostile intelligence service. This is called countersurveillance. Author Abram Shulsky gives an example of one type of countersurveillance:

> An officer may spend several hours traveling to a meeting by a circuitous route, taking several different forms of transportation. If he notices that the man who sat next to him on the westbound subway also happens to be on his eastbound bus, he may reasonably conclude that he is being followed.[12]

Other aspects of tradecraft include learning secret codes to encrypt either written messages or radio transmissions; how to conduct surveillance on another person; how to use disguises appropriately; and how to warn other agents if their covers have been compromised. During the Cold War some new officers were also taught how to argue for communism in the case of the KGB and against it in the case of the CIA. This way they could convince others of their ideology and recruit them into their service. Once the new agent learned the tradecraft necessary to gather the information the intelligence agency desired, he or she left the training facility and began work in the field.

Technical Intelligence

While some intelligence officers used agents to gather information about other nations around the world, the KGB and CIA also employed thousands of technical intelligence officers who used technology to collect information. Throughout the Cold War, technical officers were recruited from the ranks of the military as well as top universities and colleges because they exhibited skills in high-level mathematics (necessary for code breaking), computer programming, or some other scientific or technological field. Numerous people applied to work in technical intelligence each year. The National Security Agency (NSA), which intercepts the top-secret communications of other countries for the U.S. intelligence community, recruited and accepted applications from people who wished to work in computer science, cryptanalysis (code breaking), signals analysis, and intelligence analysis, among other things. The NSA's website gives their present recruiting philosophy for potential cryptanalysts:

> The NSA is looking for people who are intelligent and imaginative, and who can contribute original ideas to the solution of complex challenges. Cryptanalysts must communicate clearly, concentrate long and hard on difficult problems, and not be discouraged if success is elusive. No specific major is targeted for Cryptanalysis; the NSA hires people with technical and nontechnical degrees, ranging from mathematics to music, engineering to history, and computer programming to chemistry.[13]

Spy gadgets equipped with listening devices were developed during the Cold War.

Technical intelligence officers also were recruited throughout the Cold War to engineer gadgets for human spies as well as develop spy planes, state-of-the-art photographic equipment, and satellites. They analyzed aerial reconnaissance photographs to determine troop movements or the types of military equipment being loaded onto ships. They monitored the orbits of spy satellites and waded through mounds of data to discern important scientific, political, or technological facts. Finally, they also analyzed much of the technical information collected through both technical intelligence methods and human intelligence methods. For instance, when the KGB gathered information about a new type of weapon being developed in the United States, its technical engineers

and scientists examined the technical makeup of this weapon and assessed the threat it posed.

Getting Paid

While technical intelligence officers and case officers under official cover are paid through normal channels, one of the most unique aspects of the lives of NOCs and agents was the way in which they were paid for their work. Some NOCs simply had funds deposited into their bank accounts, but in other cases arrangements were made with a company for whom they "supposedly" worked to have their checks issued in that company's name. Just as there was a hands-off list for agents, there was a hands-off list as to which companies could be used as part of a CIA officer's cover. A general rule of thumb was that U.S. companies operating abroad could not be compromised. As a result, fake companies were often created and/or local businesses utilized to issue officers their pay.

Agents, on the other hand, were paid for the amount of information they provided, and each was paid in a unique manner. Sometimes it was just straight cash. In these instances the agent produced information and the case officer gave him or her money in exchange. Other agents requested sexual favors as payment for their information, and the agencies made arrangements for such affairs. Still other agents, especially those who worked for ideological reasons or revenge, tended to request gifts in lieu of cash payment. Agents have given away their nation's most treasured secrets and received only bottles of vodka, cigars, diamond watches, and other gifts in return. Authors Victor Marchetti and John D. Marks tell the tale of two agents who wanted only gifts. One asked for money

Recruiting Americans for the KGB

The following is an excerpt from a KGB training manual, *The Practice of Recruiting Americans in the USA and Third Countries.* The text of the manual appears in the appendix of John Barron's *KGB: The Secret Work of Secret Agents.* This passage discusses things the KGB officer should consider when trying to recruit the agent either by offering money or threatening blackmail.

It should be kept in mind that the relatively high standard of living in the U.S. is maintained by plundering the peoples of other countries. Therefore, it would be wrong to assume that an employee of a U.S. government institution can be encouraged to collaborate with Soviet intelligence for a pittance. . . .

On one hand, the money which is offered should not give the person being developed unfounded illusions that he is to receive large amounts of money for his work with us; on the other, the person under development must be firmly convinced of the readiness of our intelligence service to compensate him for services that involve the risk of losing his job in a governmental organization and of being taken to court. Obviously, a government employee who is being developed with the aim of recruitment on a material basis will not agree to collaborate with Soviet intelligence for $50 or $100 a month.

When selecting candidates for recruitment on the basis of compromising materials [blackmail], great importance is attached to information which, if revealed, could actually do serious harm to the person who is concealing it from those surrounding him. . . . It should be kept in mind that the most important information that could compromise an American consists of data on the commission of serious crimes at work, usually related to illegal appropriation of large sums of money, and also information to the effect that he is a homosexual.

once because he wished to purchase a motorboat, which he had always dreamt of owning. The other "refused all offers of pensions and political asylum in the West. He wanted only Benny Goodman records."[14]

In dealing with agents, a former DIA (Defense Intelligence Agency) case officer points out that officers "always pay the agent and always get a signature" or receipt for payment. The officer tells the agents to sign "superman or batman or any name they want," but to always sign the receipts using the same alias. That way, should an agent get cold feet and decide to stop gathering and delivering the information, the case officer can say, "Oh really? I've got six or seven signatures here that can be identified as yours through handwriting analysis"[15] and proceed to blackmail the agent into continuing to deliver information.

The Life of a Spy and Beyond

As for the spies themselves, while those involved with technology could go to work and have families just as any other government employee, the life of the case officer during the Cold War was unique. Some of them had families that knew about their work, others had families that did not know, and many officers had no spouse or children at all. For the men and women who worked as case officers in the Cold War, life after espionage was a challenge. "It's a really difficult job," said one former officer, "it really taints your life afterwards. [We are] the biggest group of alcoholics, divorcees, [and] have a high suicide rate." He added that this is because espionage is a "very sordid" profession to the point that case officers often refer to themselves as "whores." It is their job to establish meaningful relationships with perfectly kind individuals and then bribe, trick, or blackmail them into giving away the information the case officer's government wants. When the case officer gets this information, the relationship—which may have been loving and meaningful to both parties—is over. "Once you give me that file, you're nothing more than a piece of meat," the former officer says. "How many years of counseling do I need? It [messes] you up big time."[16]

Chapter 2

Cloak-and-Dagger Work in the Cold War

During the Cold War the KGB and the CIA had differing degrees of success using case officers and agents to gather information. In this type of espionage, which is sometimes called cloak-and-dagger work, the Soviets were far more successful than the CIA. Their agents and officers were able to gather information on some of the U.S. government's most carefully guarded secrets. In comparison, the United States had little or no luck penetrating the inner sanctum of Soviet society.

The KGB's success in this area was the result of a number of factors. Chief among them was the historical existence of an international intelligence organization in Russia and the Soviet Union. Basically, since a Soviet intelligence organization existed long before an American one, the KGB already had agents in place in the United States, under deep cover, when the Cold War began.

In addition, the open society of the United States was much easier to infiltrate than the closed society of the Soviet Union. Travelers and immigrants came and went in the United States every day, while it was much more difficult to travel in or immigrate to the Soviet Union. As a result, it was nearly impossible for CIA officers to get close enough to potential Soviet agents in order to recruit them. Meanwhile, it was much easier for the KGB to place NOCs in American society without arousing suspicion. Therefore, the KGB enjoyed a great deal of success in gathering information from people, especially in the early years of the Cold War when their agents and officers uncovered some of America's most carefully guarded secrets.

The Soviet Infiltration of the Manhattan Project

Perhaps the greatest Soviet achievement of this sort was their total penetration of the U.S. Manhattan Project. The Manhattan Project was the U.S. code name for a group of scientists and engineers who were working to design and develop an atomic weapon. Since possessing such a destructive weapon would give its owner an incredible military advantage, the United States knew it was important to protect the knowledge of the inner workings of the bomb—especially from the Soviets. The U.S. government took a variety of security measures to ensure the Manhattan Project's atomic weaponry information was well protected from the rest of the world. However, the KGB's agents and officers soon proved these measures were nowhere near sufficient to stop their espionage.

When the United States bombed Hiroshima and Nagasaki in August of 1945, it announced its ability to build an atomic weapon to the world—particularly to the Soviets. The fact that the United States had a working bomb and the Soviets did not, greatly upset Joseph Stalin, the Soviet leader, who feared for the safety of his country. "A single demand of you, comrades!" Stalin told the

An immigrant to the United States is sworn in by a special Board of Enquiry in 1950. The United States was much easier to penetrate during the Cold War than was Russia.

group of Soviet scientists working on the Soviet atomic bomb. "Provide us with atomic weapons in the shortest possible time! You know that Hiroshima has shaken the whole world. The balance [of power] has been destroyed!"[17]

Stalin knew this should not take too terribly long since the Soviet scientists pretty much knew everything there was to know about how the American weapon worked. Their information had come not just from their own scientific research, but also from very effective espionage. The first spy to supply Moscow with scientific intelligence on U.S. atomic research was Klaus Fuchs. Born

in Germany, Fuchs joined the German Communist Party (KPD) in 1932 but had to flee Germany for his Communist beliefs after Hitler's rise to power in 1933. Fuchs went to England, where he got his Ph.D. in physics in 1936. In 1941 he became part of the British top-secret Tube Alloys project, the British code name for their program to design and build an atomic weapon. The British were hesitant to grant Fuchs security clearance to work on the project since he was still in-

Klaus Fuchs (bottom right) was the first KGB spy to supply Moscow with information about the top secret U.S. Manhattan Project (pictured).

volved with the German Communist underground movement in England. However, at the request of his friend Rudolph Peierls, for whom he would work, they eventually agreed. As it turns out, the British should have heeded the warning signs because in the same year Fuchs went to work on the Tube Alloys project, he volunteered his services to the Soviets as a spy because of his belief in communism. His offer was graciously accepted, and his value to the Soviets only increased when in 1944 Fuchs became one of several Tube Alloys scientists working on the U.S. Manhattan Project.

Fuchs passed a great deal of information about fissionable uranium, which is considered the key to the atomic bomb, to the KGB through his controller, Raymond. Their first meeting in the United States was the stuff that Hollywood movies are made of. So they would recognize each other, Fuchs, carrying a tennis ball in his hand, set off to meet a man wearing one pair of gloves while carrying a second pair as well as a green-covered book. At their meeting, Fuchs told Raymond about the U.S. scientists' work on the production of fissionable uranium. With his divulgence of this highly protected information, Fuchs opened the door to U.S. atomic information for the Soviets.

While he may not have known it, Fuchs was not the only Soviet agent who had access to the Manhattan Project. Donald Maclean was a KGB officer who worked as the first secretary of the British embassy in Washington, D.C. Maclean was also a member of the Combined Policy Committee that coordinated the joint U.S.–British-Canadian effort to build an atomic weapon. Maclean's position on the Combined Policy Committee gave Moscow important information about the progress of the Western allies in their quest for atomic capability and, later, American atomic strength.

In addition to Fuchs and Maclean, an American named David Greenglass provided engineering information to the Soviets. Greenglass was a twenty-two-year-old who worked as a machinist on the Manhattan Project. He was also the brother of Ethel Rosenberg who, along with her husband Julius, was part of a KGB spy ring in New York. Greenglass and the Rosenbergs all believed in communism, and Ethel and Julius appealed to Greenglass's desire to be a good Communist when convincing him to supply information about the Manhattan Project. Greenglass was an army sergeant who worked on parts of the bomb for testing. In January 1945, while he was in New York, Greenglass gave Julius Rosenberg numerous notes and sketches from inside the Los Alamos machine shop where the parts were produced. Greenglass met with Soviet controllers at least two more times and continued to provide them with valuable information about the engineering aspects of the bomb.

Finally, the Soviets also had a key agent working on the Manhattan Project team based in Canada, a British scientist named Allan Nunn May. May was a Communist and became a goldmine of intelligence for the Soviets. Author Christopher Andrew explains, "On August 9, 1945, three days after Hiroshima, [May] gave Angelov [his KGB controller] a report on atomic research, details of the bomb dropped on Hiroshima, and two samples of uranium: an enriched specimen of U-235 in a glass tube and a thin deposit of U-233 on a piece of platinum foil."[18] In return, May received a bottle of whiskey and two-hundred Canadian dollars, which was sufficient since May believed he was contributing to "the safety of mankind"[19] and saw espionage as a duty.

The combination of the scientific information gathered by Fuchs and May, the engineering information from Greenglass, and Maclean's reports on the progress of the Manhattan Project, provided the Soviets with a fairly complete picture of the U.S.–British–Canadian bomb-building program. As a result, long before President Truman officially told Stalin about the existence of a working atomic weapon at Potsdam in 1945, the Soviet leader knew of it through the expansive Soviet espionage efforts. While it would take a few more years for the Soviets to create their own atomic weapon, the intelligence gathered by the KGB's agents and officers greatly accelerated the process.

From "Leaf" to "VADIM": Top Secret

The following is an excerpt from an originally top-secret KGB document that explains the contents of a report given by Maclean (code-name Leaf) to A.V. Gorsky (codename VADIM), head of the Soviet intelligence ring in London. It is contained in the appendix of Pavel and Anatoli Sudoplatov's book, *Special Tasks: The Memoirs of an Unwanted Witness—a Soviet Spymaster*, and lends insight into just how much information Maclean was in a position to give the KGB.

TOP SECRET Report

On No. 7073, 7081/1096 of October 3, 1941, from London

VADIM informs about a report, received from Leaf, which was submitted to the War Cabinet on September 24, 1941, on pro-jects of the Uranium Committee. The report touches on the following issues:

The calculation of the critical mass depends on determining the fission cross section of the uranium 235 nucleus. It is assumed that the amount of the critical mass lies between 10 and 43 kilograms. This amount was determined on the basis of general information about the properties of U-235 and the impact of high-velocity neutrons on atoms of other elements.

The production of uranium hexafluoride has been developed by Imperial Chemical Industries, which has already obtained 3 kilograms of the substance. The production of [U-235] is effected by way of diffusion of uranium hexafluoride in a gaseous state through a number of membranes which are grids of the finest wire.

The Magnificent Five

Another Soviet feat in HUMINT was their recruitment and running of the five officers who became known as the Magnificent Five or the Cambridge Five. Recruited by Arnold Deutch for the KGB from Cambridge University in the early 1930s, Kim Philby, Anthony Blunt, Donald Maclean, Guy Burgess, and John Cairncross went on to become powerful members of British society. Philby was the most successful. He became the Secret Intelligence Service (SIS, the British intelligence agency) station commander in Washington, D.C., and before he was found out, it looked as though he might one day be named the Chief of the British Secret Service. As station commander, he had access to extremely high-level information in both the British and U.S. governments.

Philby's associates, Donald Maclean and Guy Burgess, also held key positions in the British government and intelligence agency. Therefore, they too had access to protected information. Maclean entered the British Foreign Office in 1935 and held high-level positions such as head of the American Department of the Foreign Office in London, which allowed him to keep close tabs on the Manhattan Project. Burgess was both a British intelligence officer and a member of the Foreign Office during his time as an active KGB agent.

While Guy Burgess held some important positions throughout his career that

KGB spy Kim Philby achieved the rank of SIS commander before he was suspected of espionage in 1951.

allowed him to give the KGB highly protected information, he was perhaps most important for his ability to spot potential recruits. It was Burgess who spotted Maclean and put him in touch with Deutch. He also is credited with bringing in the fourth of the Five, Anthony Blunt. Blunt went on from Cambridge to enter the British Security Service (MI5). From this position he supplied the KGB with a great deal of information during the Second World War and beyond. He was also responsible for recruiting the fifth of the Magnificent Five, John Cairncross.

John Cairncross was briefly a member of the Foreign Office, and the KGB hoped he would penetrate this organization.

However, Cairncross's disagreeable personality seems to have gotten in the way—he had difficulty making friends and, therefore, gaining access to information. After a year in the Foreign Office, Cairncross transferred to the Treasury Department and, in part because of his position, was very successful as a KGB officer in this department. He provided his controllers with a wealth of information from his positions in the Defence (Material) and Defence (Personnel) divisions of the treasury. "Though Cairncross is the last of the Five to be publicly identified, he successfully penetrated a greater variety of the corridors of power and intelligence than any of the other four," Christopher Andrew writes in *KGB: The Inside Story*. Andrew adds, "In less than a decade after leaving Cambridge, he served successively in the Foreign Office, the Treasury, the private office of a government minister, the sigint agency GC & CS [Government Code & Cypher School], and SIS"[20] all the while working as an agent for the KGB.

The Magnificent Five provided the KGB with a great deal of information from the early 1940s through 1951. They were by far the most important foreign intelligence officers the KGB had during this time. However, in 1951 Burgess and Maclean were discovered and fled to Moscow. After the cover of these two men was compromised, the U.S. Joint Chiefs of Staff (JCS) assessed the threat their access to information had posed for U.S. security. The JCS concluded, "Insofar as U.S. security implications are concerned it would appear that very nearly all U.S./U.K. high level planning information prior to 25 May 1951 must be considered compromised."[21] However, the

Marxism Hits Cambridge

The November 1973 issue of *Studio International* contained an article titled "From Bloomsbury to Marxism" written by Anthony Blunt (one of the Magnificent Five). In it Blunt recalled his introduction to Marxism at Cambridge. It was his belief in this ideology that, in part, motivated his work as a KGB agent. It was this sort of ideological commitment to their cause that both agencies looked for in potential recruits since these sorts of individuals typically made the best agents.

Then, quite suddenly, in the autumn term of 1933, Marxism hit Cambridge. I can date it precisely because I had sabbatical leave for that term, and when I came back in January I found that almost all my younger friends had become Marxists and joined the Communist Party; and Cambridge was literally transformed overnight. Marxism had hit Oxford a good deal earlier but not nearly so hard. . . . The older ones were not affected by the wave of Marxism, and generally speaking even the younger fellows were little touched, but the undergraduates and graduate students were swept away by it and during the next three or four years almost every intelligent undergraduate who came up to Cambridge joined the Communist Party at some time during his first year.

JCS took no further action except to "ask around" about whom the KGB might have in place to take the place of these two agents.

At the time Burgess and Maclean were discovered to be spies, Cairncross was under suspicion and forced to resign from the Treasury, and Philby was under suspicion and forced to resign from the SIS. Suddenly, the KGB lost access to a great deal of information. Soon after Philby was dismissed in 1951, the KGB recruited another SIS officer, George Blake. While Blake was a very driven officer, he was never as effective as the man he replaced. He continued to operate throughout the 1950s betraying American and British agents to the KGB left and right until he was caught in April 1961.

Walker Family Spy Ring

The next great Soviet achievement in HUMINT came in late 1967 with U.S. Navy chief warrant officer John Walker, a communications officer on the staff of the commander of submarine forces in the Atlantic. Walker was a "walk-in," which means he sought out the KGB, they did not have to recruit him. He walked into the Soviet Embassy and declared, "I'm a naval officer. I'd like to make some money and I'll give you some genuine stuff in return."[22] And Walker had a great deal of important information to offer. He had "crypto" code clearance, which meant he had access to the U.S. Navy's top-secret codes and could give the Sovi-

ets insight into the conversations and movements of the U.S. naval fleet, including the well-protected *Trident* and *Polaris* nuclear missile submarines.

Walker was not at all like the Magnificent Five. The Five believed in communism and wanted to be true KGB officers. Walker, on the other hand, was a mercenary agent who would do anything for money. Author Christopher Andrew describes Walker:

> His criminal career had begun early. He joined the navy as a teenage high school dropout to escape punishment after four serious burglaries. When he got into debt after the failure of business ventures, he tried to force his wife into prostitution to restore his finances. Walker drew his family into work for the KGB. When his daughter's pregnancy threatened to interfere with his espionage, he tried to persuade her to have an abortion.[23]

Walker's primary asset seems to have been his charm and ability to manipulate people. Ironically, he received glowing reviews from his superiors testifying to his intense loyalty. In his work for the KGB, Walker recruited his brother Arthur who was a lieutenant commander and antisubmarine specialist; his son Michael who was a crewman on the naval ship *Nimitz;* and Jerry Whitworth, Walker's friend and a retired senior radioman. Together the four men provided the Soviets with keys

A U.S. nuclear submarine is loaded with Polaris missiles in 1960.

to U.S. naval communications for nearly two decades. Walker's cover was blown when his ex-wife reported him to the FBI in 1985.

U.S. Achievements in Spying

In comparison to the KGB, the CIA's achievements in the area of gathering intelligence from agents were quite modest. It was difficult for the United States to make contact with individuals who might be willing to give them protected information because the countries that made up the Soviet Bloc had closed societies.

Hundreds of thousands of people immigrate to the United States each year, and an even greater number of travelers set foot on its soil. As a result, the KGB found it relatively easy to place officers and agents in the United States. Disguised as immigrants or travelers, they could enter easily without being noticed. Traveling or immigrating to the USSR or Soviet Bloc was an entirely different matter. Borders were heavily guarded, passports continually checked, and the KGB watched some travelers closely. These factors made it very difficult for the CIA either to sneak an officer into the Soviet Union or make contact with potential agents who resided within its borders.

Therefore, most of the information that the CIA was able to gather from people who had access to Soviet secrets came from defectors and walk-ins who actively sought out the CIA or an intelligence agency of a U.S. ally. One such walk-in was Igor Gouzenko, who sought asylum in Canada for himself, his wife, and his child. In September 1945 Gouzenko stuffed a bunch of top-secret documents under his shirt and walked out of the Soviet embassy in Moscow. His wife later explained that he had to suck in his stomach as he made his way out of the embassy because "otherwise . . . he would have looked pregnant."[24] The information Gouzenko provided helped the CIA identify a major GRU (*Glavnoye Razvedyvatelnoye Upravlenie*, Soviet military intelligence, which is a separate organization from the KGB) spy ring called Operation Candy, which included a number of important Canadian military officers and government officials. Further investigation of the members of the spy ring helped lead officials to scientists Allan Nunn May and Klaus Fuchs. Realizing that top scientists such as these were passing information to the GRU, the United States and Great Britain finally came to understand that the Soviets had skillfully obtained top-secret information on the Manhattan Project and the atomic bomb.

While the exposure of Operation Candy was problematic for the KGB, even more troublesome for the Soviets was the fact that Gouzenko had escaped with invaluable codebooks and was himself a code clerk who could give officials insight into the ciphering systems used by the Soviets. Gouzenko's codebooks became one of many keys the United States used to gain insight into an "unbreakable" code used by the Soviets to transmit important intelligence communications.

A walk-in named Pyotr Semyonovich Popov provided the United States with another information breakthrough. Popov was a major in the GRU and became the first military officer ever recruited by the CIA. According to author Nathan Miller, Popov contacted the CIA because of a "festering anger at Soviet exploitation of the Russian peasantry from which he came."[25] From the day he was recruited in 1952 until he was discovered and executed by the Soviets in 1958, Popov provided the CIA with "trundled bales of top-secret information out of the secret centers of Soviet power," according to William Hood, deputy chief of the CIA station in Vienna. "In the process, he shattered the Soviet military intelligence service, caused the transfer of the KGB chief . . . and saved the United States half a billion dollars in military research."[26]

A third U.S. espionage triumph came when the CIA secured a copy of Nikita

Khrushchev's speech given before the Twentieth Congress of the Communist Party. Khrushchev had succeeded Stalin as the premier of the Soviet Union. In February 1956 his speech to the Party gave a detailed account of Stalin's brutal actions and even went so far as to condemn some of them. Allegedly through Mossad, the Israeli intelligence agency, the CIA was able to obtain a copy of the speech in exchange for money and technology. The speech was eventually leaked to the *New York Times* and published. This publication allowed China as well as several Soviet satellite nations to learn of the brutality of Stalin's regime, and it is credited with increasing tension between the Soviet Union and these countries, most notably Poland and Hungary.

KGB *Yavkas*

The Mitrokhin archive includes a list of some of the KGB's favorite meeting places, or *yavkas*, in the United States in the 1960s. At these spots, agents would meet their handlers, and pass information.

Baltimore: by the Clayton men's clothing store on North Avenue.

Boston: the music hall; by the State Hilton Hotel.

Chicago: the Chicago Institute of Fine Arts buildings.

Cleveland: by the Khipp movie theater.

Indianapolis: by the notice board on Market Street.

Los Angeles: by the newspaper stand "Out of Town Papers" on Las Palmas Avenue.

Newark: by the Newark train station, on the bench by the monument to Sergeant Donan A Bazilone.

New Haven: by the Taft Hotel; by the Sherman movie theater.

New York: (Bronx): by the David Marcus movie theater; by the restaurant Savarin.

Philadelphia: by the Randolph and Stanton movie theaters; by the Silvanna Hotel.

Portland: by the parking lot on the main street; by the Parker movie theater.

Rochester: by the Randolph movie theater.

Sacramento: by the Tower movie theater, and near the advertisements at the café Camilia Lodge.

St. Paul: by the display windows of the St. Paul Hotel; by the Strand movie theater.

San Francisco: by the Metro movie theater on Union Street; by Fosters restaurant, Simms Café, and Comptons Café (in the downtown area); the Canterbury Hotel.

Seattle: by the movie theater Orpheum Cinema on Fifth Avenue; by the City Motel on Queen Anne Avenue.

Syracuse: by the Cates movie theater.

Union City, NJ: by the A&P supermarket.

Washington DC area: the telephone booth by the entrance to the Hot Shoppes Restaurant in the center of Hyattsville, a Washington suburb; by the entrance to the grocery store in the Aspen Hill Shopping Center on Georgia Avenue in Maryland, six miles north of Washington DC.

Former Soviet Premier Nikita Khrushchev delivers a speech to the National Press Club in 1959.

However, the political effects of the printing of the speech were minimal, and in the end it was more of a public relations triumph. It allowed the United States to gloat about successful espionage as well as condemn the terrible crimes of Stalin, which, in turn, embarrassed the Soviets.

Over the course of the Cold War, U.S. case officers and the agents they handled provided the CIA with access to additional, top-secret Soviet information. The United States worked with the British to run an agent who was a colonel in the GRU, Oleg Vladimirovich Penkovsky. Penkovsky provided the United States and Great Britain with high-grade intelligence until his capture in 1962, after which he was tortured, sentenced to death at a show trial (a trial in which the guilt of the person has already been decided, and the trial is put on for show) in Moscow in May 1963, and shot soon thereafter. In addition to Penkovsky, the United States continued to attract walk-ins and defectors who provided information in the latter years of the Cold War. However, unlike the Soviets who could easily penetrate U.S. society or the SIS, the United States could not depend on infiltrating Soviet society through espionage. Other means of infiltrating the secret alcoves of Soviet society had to be found, and technology offered the answer.

⋆ Chapter 3 ⋆

Technology and the Changing Role of the Spy

As the Cold War progressed, technological advances continued to alter the world of espionage. Scientists developed machines to collect information from thousands of miles away that was formerly gathered by spies on the scene. Intelligence agencies built and launched satellites to collect data similar to that which was once painstakingly gathered by networks of spies. And even when officers and agents were directly involved in information collection, technology greatly improved the tools at their disposal.

Spy Gadgets

At the start of the Cold War cameras were big, copy machines did not exist, and handheld microphones were considered state of the art. In 1945 a tape recorder of any size seemed downright revolutionary. However, in today's world where there are cameras that fit on pencil tips, it is hard to imagine a time when a spy would have

had to take out a big clunky camera to photograph a document. It is equally difficult to imagine an officer or agent trying to conceal even a small tape recorder. Today's spies go into the game with amazing tools at their disposal—virtually undetectable audio devices, cameras so small that it is difficult for the human eye to see them, and other nearly unbelievable gadgets. The development of many of these tools that are used in espionage began during the Cold War.

The Technical Services Division (TSD) of the CIA and the Directorates of Operational Technical Support and Science and Technology of the FCD created tools for the use of operatives throughout the Cold War. In 1974 Victor Marchetti and John D. Marks wrote about the "dazzling" unusual paraphernalia available for clandestine operations:

A signal transmitter disguised as a false tooth, a pencil which looks and writes like an ordinary pencil but can also write invisibly on special paper, a bizarre automobile rearview mirror that allows the driver to observe not the traffic behind but the occupants of the back seat instead.[27]

In 1974, gadgets such as these seemed to be marvels of modern technology.

However, these high-tech devices proved useful only under very specific sets of circumstances, and as a result some of the more imaginative gadgets cooked up by the TSD and the Directorate of Science and Technology during the Cold War had very little impact in real operations. The technological advances that had the most significant impact were those that could be widely used in any number of situations. For this reason, advances in audio, video, and communications encryption were more far-reaching because they made the lives of a large number of espionage officers much easier and safer.

Fear of a Soviet Surprise Attack

Technology not only altered the tools used by spies, it also revolutionized the

Modern technical devices allow spies to gather intelligence undetected.

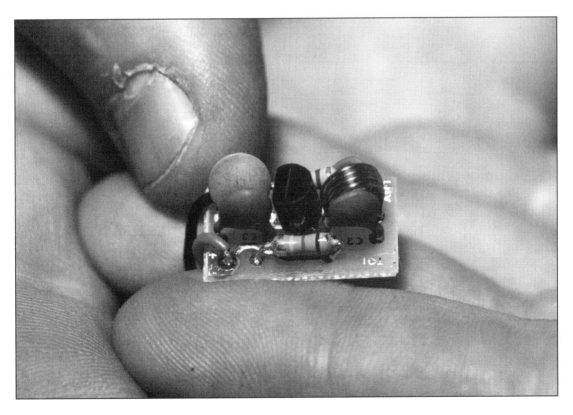

way in which information was gathered. The motivating factor behind the development of technology throughout the Cold War was fear, the fear of a surprise attack. For the United States this fear intensified when the Soviets successfully exploded an atomic weapon in 1949.

Envisioning a surprise attack of Soviet bombers heading toward the United States and Western Europe carrying nuclear weapons, the U.S. military searched for a solution. Since the best way to defend against the element of surprise is to know what is coming, they surmised that some sort of early warning system was the best possible answer.

Watchers

The United States and the USSR used intelligence officers to such an end in World War II. Called "watchers," they infiltrated Germany, Japan, Italy, and other enemy nations and set up shop near military bases. When they saw signs that troops were preparing for battle—by readying a number of planes, boats, or other unusual activities—the watcher contacted his or her home country via radio and warned them of the impending assault.

After World War II ended, the KGB continued to use watchers to monitor U.S. air bases and warn Moscow in the event of a surprise attack. Thus, the obvious solution for America's problem was to infiltrate watchers into the Soviet Union. The military concluded that since there were hundreds of Soviet air bases,

hundreds of CIA intelligence officers would need to be set up in the USSR with cover and radio communications capabilities immediately. The CIA knew this would be impossible. They had difficulty infiltrating just one officer into Soviet society. The idea of sending in hundreds of agents at a time was laughable. Given the harsh reality that the CIA did not have the capability to infiltrate the Soviet Union with intelligence officers, the CIA and the military turned to aerial reconnaissance to solve their problem.

Aerial Reconnaissance

Aerial reconnaissance (which literally means to scout or search by air for information that can be used for military purposes) relies on high-tech aviation and photographic equipment to collect information secretly. A plane flies over an area taking pictures which are later analyzed by specialists to determine the contents of the photographs. This sort of monitoring system allows intelligence agencies to see troops moving, warplanes readying for takeoff, and the movements of naval fleets. At the beginning of the Cold War the United States used a plane called the RB-47 for aerial reconnaissance. It was a B-47 bomber equipped with state-of-the-art photographic equipment, and it was capable of taking very clear, detailed pictures of any part of the Soviet Union.

However, countries do not generally allow their adversaries to fly over their

A Naval officer examines photographs of a Soviet spy vessel taken during a 1968 aerial reconnaissance mission.

nation taking detailed military photographs at will. In fact, international law prohibits flying over another country without its consent. Any flight in violation of this law can legally be shot down. Not wanting to risk being shot down from the skies, at the onset of the Cold War the U.S. RB-47 flew along the borders of the USSR taking photographs a short distance inside. The United States dared not fly into the vast expanse inside the Soviet Union where Russian MIG fighter jets could intercept the RB-47

and shoot it down. In 1950, after the Soviets developed surface-to-air missiles (SAMs), which could reach an altitude of sixty thousand feet (higher than any known aircraft could fly), flying aircraft over the USSR to gather information became all the riskier.

During this period the Soviets also achieved nuclear capability, making it all the more important to gather information about the strength of their forces and be able to spot a surprise attack. Clearly, the United States was going to have to find some new way to spy on the Soviets. The CIA tried many strange and different ways of gathering this information. Author Abram Shulsky explains one such plan:

> One project, code-named Moby Dick, involved launching balloons equipped with downward-pointing cameras in Western Europe. The plan was that these balloons would then drift across the Soviet Union on the prevailing westerly winds until they reached Japan or the Pacific Ocean. At that point, their camera pods would be released in response to a radio signal and recovered. In reality, many balloons came down over the Soviet Union, enabling the Soviets to assess the camera's technology.[28]

After other equally problematic solutions were tried and failed, a presidential committee suggested the development of a plane that would fly at high altitudes out of the reach of MIG fighters and SAMs and be equipped with state-of-the-art photographic equipment. In 1954 the

The Capture of Francis Gary Powers

The following excerpt appeared in *Time Magazine* on May 16, 1960, and details U-2 flights, the capture of Francis Gary Powers, and Khrushchev's reaction. The Soviet capture of Powers and his plane marked the end of U-2 flights over the country.

As the world found out last week, Francis Powers, onetime U.S. Air Force first lieutenant, was off on an intrepid flight that would ultimately carry him up the spine of the Soviet Union. From south to north, his high-flying instruments would record the effectiveness of Russian radar, sample the air for radioactive evidence of illicit nuclear tests. The U-2's sensitive infra-red cameras could sweep vast arcs of landscape, spot tall, thin smokestacks or rocket blasts—if there were any—on pads far below.

Francis Powers was on an intelligence mission, like many unsung pilots before him. . . .

But Pilot Powers had bad luck: he got caught, and Soviet Premier Nikita Khrushchev says that he talked. Thus Khrushchev had the chance to tell the world about the U-2's mission last week—with all the embellishment and distortion that best suited his case.

[According to Khrushchev] on May 1, [Powers] took off on a reconnaissance flight that was supposed to take him up the Ural Mountains to Murmansk. . . . Soviet radar tracked him all the way, and over Sverdlovsk on Khrushchev's personal order, he was shot down at 65,000 ft. by a Soviet ground-to-air rocket [SAM]. Pilot Powers, said Khrushchev, declined to fire his ejection seat because that would have blown up his plane, its instrumentation and possibly Powers himself. Instead, he climbed out of his cockpit, parachuted to earth and was captured while his plane crashed nearby.

CIA was placed in charge of this new plane's development.

Spies in the Sky

Richard M. Bissell, who was the head of the CIA at the time, assigned the task of building a new plane that could fly at high altitude to Clarence L. "Kelly" Johnson of Lockheed Aircraft. For the powerful photographic equipment Bissell called on Edwin Land, who invented the Polaroid camera. In 1956, less than two years later (and four years ahead of schedule), the first U-2 spy plane was completed, fitted with photographic equipment, and ready to go in search of Soviet secrets.

The plane flew at seventy thousand feet, ten thousand feet above the reach of the Soviet SAMs. It was well out of the range of MIG fighters, and it was said that the clarity of the images taken by the photographic equipment made it possible to make out the models of the cars in the parking lot at the Kremlin or see the golf ball being used by President Eisenhower. U-2s were also equipped with radio interception devices to collect signals intelligence for the National Security Agency.

Beginning in 1956, U-2s flew over the Soviet Union at will, taking pictures of missile silos, air bases, and nuclear test facilities. There was nothing the KGB or the Soviet government could do about these high-flying spies, not because they did not know about them, but because

complaining to the international community about the illegality of the flights would mean the Soviets would have to admit to having inferior technology.

The success of the U-2 spy plane was the first in a long line of advances that, through the use of newly developed technologies, could provide intelligence agencies with information formerly collected by spies on the scene. Watchers were no longer necessary within the borders of adversaries. Troop movements and preparations for a surprise attack could be seen from the skies. In addition, a great deal of information about the military and nuclear capabilities of the Soviets could be gleaned from photographs. Much of this information quelled U.S. officials' fears about a Soviet missile buildup.

Since such important military and nuclear capability information could be gathered through the skies, it diminished the need for case officers and agents to attempt to infiltrate the corridors of power in the USSR to get this information. "By 1959," write Ernest Volkman and Blaine Baggett, "the U-2 photographs and signals collected . . . by detection gear inside the spy planes provided nearly 90 percent of all intelligence on the Soviet Union."[29]

From the Skies to Space

In 1960 the Soviets developed the technology to stop U-2 flights. Their new SAM missiles reached altitudes over seventy

The Problems and Importance of CORONA

Discoverer was actually a codename for the CORONA spy satellite. In the following excerpt from Paul Hoversten's article, "CORONA: Celebrating 40 Years of Spy Satellites," which appears at www.space.com, describes the difficulties its creators faced and the importance of its success. The documents regarding the project were declassified in 1995.

> [The] CORONA [program] itself was fraught with difficulty, [Retired Air Force colonel Richard] Leghorn recalled. "If it hadn't been for Eisenhower staying with it, it never would have happened. We had a new booster, the Thor, and a new satellite, the Agena. Then you had a camera that had never been built before, with film that was completely new. Add to that the fact that you had to grab the package from the air.
>
> "All those elements were new and to get them to work together was really a fantastic achievement. It was a very hairy exercise. . . . If you'd had today's process of review committees, CORONA wouldn't have lasted beyond two or three failures," Leghorn said.

> CORONA in fact suffered 12 straight failures before the 13th flight worked. But that flight lacked a camera so it wasn't until the 14th mission—on August 18, 1960—that CORONA was successful.
>
> To get the film home, the satellite had to drop a capsule with the film toward Earth. Then, two small parachutes on the capsule opened to slow its speed. Finally, an Air Force C-119 aircraft swooped in to snatch the capsule in midair and returned it to Earth where CIA and Air Force technicians processed the film. . . .
>
> In all, the CORONA program involved more than 100 satellite flights from 1960 to 1972 at a cost of about $850 million.
>
> The imagery allowed the U.S. intelligence community to catalog Soviet air defense and antiballistic missile sites, nuclear weapons-related facilities and submarine bases along with military installations in China and Eastern Europe. CORONA also provided pictures in the 1967 Arab-Israeli war and Soviet arms control compliance.

thousand feet, high enough to shoot down the CIA's U-2 spies from the skies. On May 1, 1960, the Soviets shot down a U-2 flight piloted by a CIA contract employee named Francis Gary Powers. This was the last known U-2 flight made over the Soviet Union. Powers was sentenced to a ten-year term for espionage in the USSR, and the United States needed a new way to gather information about the Soviets.

Fortunately, a solution was already in the works. Bissell had anticipated that Soviet technology would catch up with, and

eventually ground, the U-2 spy plane. To counteract this, as early as 1958 the United States had begun work on a satellite with photoreconnaissance capabilities. It was rough going, and twelve successive missions failed to produce results. However, a few months after Powers's U-2 flight was brought down, the United States launched *Discoverer XIV*, its first successful spy satellite. This new technology could easily outrange any Soviet missile as it hurtled through outer space crisscrossing the globe and photographing the world below. In his article, "CORONA: Celebrating 40 Years of Spy Satellites," Paul Hoversten discusses the important advance in intelligence collection that *Discoverer XIV* signaled, "In a single day, [*Discoverer XIV*] yielded more images of the Soviet Union than did the entire U-2 spy plane program."[30]

The photos provided by *Discoverer XIV* lacked the clarity and definition of those of the U-2, but as time went on, photo quality improved. In 1961, with the launch of *Samos 2*, U.S. satellites were also equipped with the ability to intercept radio and television signals. By the end of 1963 the Soviets had their own spy satellite orbiting the earth photographing the United States and listening to its communications. Now, information that had previously been gathered by the people who spied for the CIA and the KGB was being collected from

outer space by high-tech machinery. A new day had dawned in the world of espionage.

Downgrading the Importance of Cloak-and-Dagger Work

The new technology greatly affected HUMINT, especially for the United States. Now, through the aid of technology, the United States could see and hear into a country that previously had been a complete enigma. The CIA decided to throw a great deal of its resources behind sustaining and developing new technologies and to downgrade the importance of running foreign agents. This sparked controversy, and two camps developed within the agency. One camp believed technological intelligence collection was the most important

Sputnik, the first Soviet satellite launched into space, on display in 1957.

High-Tech Killing Tools

In the spring of 1954 Nikolai Khokhlov, a well-trained KGB assassin, defected to the CIA. At a press conference, he offered American reporters a peek into the gadgets then being used in the world of espionage. The following is a description of the high-tech killing device with which the KGB equipped Khokhlov. It appeared in *Newsweek* on May 3, 1954:

> These weapons were ingenious precision instruments for killing quietly. Two of them were three-barreled pistols, 4 inches long. Two others were fake cigarette cases; when the leather base was pressed, a tiny battery discharged a dumdum bullet, containing 100 times as much potassium cyanide as is needed to kill.

type of information gathering and argued that it would only continue to become increasingly more important as time went on. When the CIA had a Director of Central Intelligence (DCI) who adhered to this line of thinking, case officers were laid off in large numbers.

Admiral Stansfield Turner was one such DCI. In the late 1970s, "He . . . 'retired' seven hundred CIA officers, mostly in the Operations Directorate—home of human spies—on the grounds that increasingly expensive intelligence systems made such cuts mandatory," Ernest Volkman explains. Stansfield's argument was "the CIA could either have large staffs of human spies or it could have highly complex and costly technical systems, but not both."[31] When the case intelligence offi-

cers complained, Stansfield replied that they were just outdated old-timers who did not understand.

A second camp argued that the importance of technical intelligence gathering was being exaggerated. They believed that a balance between the two types of collection was necessary. In the end, they proved to be closer to the mark. While technology allows intelligence agencies to closely monitor the farthest reaches of the globe, too much information without any way to prioritize or evaluate it can be a significant problem. It is important to know which information to pay attention to and which information to ignore. Only human beings can distinguish between them. Those who adhered to this line of thinking also pointed out that when technical equipment malfunctioned or was compromised it would take a great deal of time and money to replace it. On the other hand, it did not cost much to replace a compromised officer or agent.

Thus, while CIA insiders argued about the role that technological intelligence should play in the agency, no one ever doubted its importance or that it had revolutionized espionage. However, it was not merely the photographs taken by U-2s and satellites that were valuable. Equally important were the radio and television signals that were being recorded. Studying these, along with other types of intercepted communications, led to significant intelligence breakthroughs throughout the Cold War.

Chapter 4

Listening In: Communications Intelligence During the Cold War

Communications intelligence refers to the gathering of information by listening in on the secret conversations of the adversary. Throughout the Cold War, the agents of First Chief Directorate of the KGB supplied Moscow with information that was far better than that which their American counterparts could provide to the CIA. However, the U.S. intelligence organization leveled the playing field by having superior communications intelligence capabilities.

While there are numerous ways to listen in on conversations, the most obvious is to try to overhear them. Following this logic, intelligence agencies "bug" rooms in which important conversations occur by planting minuscule microphones in places they cannot be detected. This way, they can overhear what is said in the room.

Bugs

The KGB's most successful communications intelligence achievements came from placing listening devices in, or bugging, rooms in which important conversations dealing with high-level intelligence took place. They were able to utilize their skilled agents to plant bugs in the offices of important British and U.S. officials. Before the Cold War even began, opposing intelligence ferreted out bugs the KGB had planted anywhere and everywhere. With the discovery of these listening devices, it became clear to other intelligence organizations that the Soviets had the capability to listen in on some high-level conversations of the CIA and the SIS as well as the British and U.S. governments.

The actual listening devices came in all different shapes and sizes and were hidden in imaginative places. Tiny microphones could be placed in the legs of tables and chairs. They could be hidden in pictures, plants, plaques, or pencils. Some were built into the walls of the building. When intelligence organizations began to

sweep for bugs and locate them by the metallic materials used in their construction, clever communications intelligence officers suggested they be built into walls behind radiators so that the radiators, which were also metal, would make it impossible to find the listening device without first thinking to remove the radiator.

Throughout the Cold War, the KGB successfully planted bugs in a number of foreign embassies with differing results. The first American embassy in Moscow came into being in 1933, and eleven years later, when the Americans conducted an electronic sweep to check for listening devices, they were surprised to find 120 microphones discreetly hidden through-

A Soviet transmitter confiscated by the CIA in 1967.

out the building. When a new American embassy was under construction in Moscow in 1953, the CIA knew from experience the KGB would try to plant listening devices in it. Therefore, the organization placed U.S. security officers around the construction site to stave off any attempts. Determined to make the new embassy bug-free, security personnel stood guard each day. Unfortunately for the Americans, no one stood guard at night, and the KGB was able to bug the new embassy. In hindsight, the U.S. officials admitted that guarding the embassy only during the day was shortsighted.

The KGB also successfully planted listening devices in the British SIS station in Beirut, Lebanon, Britain's most strategic station in the Middle East. In 1964 they convinced a maid named Elizabeth Aghasapet Ghazarian to become a KGB agent and had her place listening devices in the embassy. By listening to the goings-on of the residence, the KGB learned the identities of more than fifty SIS agents who were operating undercover in the KGB and GRU. They also learned that the British had infiltrated the Lebanese Communist Party. The microphones planted by Ghazarian (alias ZOLUSHKA) remained in place for nearly seven years before they were discovered by the SIS and removed.

For a room or building to remain bugged for seven years is rare, especially today with the technology available to detect listening devices. The short-term nature of this sort of communications intelligence is one of its major drawbacks. Typically, it is only a matter of days, months, or a couple years before listening devices are detected and disposed of. Another drawback to this type of communications intelligence is that it relies on case officers and agents to plant the device, and this puts them at risk. Once the bug is found, the cover of either the agent, the officer, or both will be blown. To avoid these problems, intelligence agencies have found other ways to listen in on conversations.

Intercepting Radio Conversations

Another way to listen in on a conversation is to intercept it. In World War II and the Cold War, spies, the military, and diplomats used radio transmissions to send information as quickly as possible. While the speed with which information could be transmitted by radio was an advantage, the disadvantage was that anyone tuned into the proper frequency could listen in on, or intercept, the conversation. Intercepting highly confidential radio transmissions quickly became an important part of communications intelligence. In an effort to keep sensitive transmissions secret, intelligence agencies and governments developed various codes and encoded their transmissions prior to sending them. This way, if a rival intelligence agency did intercept their transmission, they would have no idea what was actually being said.

The use of codes, or ciphers, to transmit information via radio waves did stop rival agencies from understanding conversations to some degree, but cryptanalysts found ways to break codes. When this occurred, a country's adversaries could listen to and understand its most top-secret conversations. Also, the opposing intelligence organization could use a spy's radio to pretend to be an agent's legitimate controller and either transmit false information or trick the agent into identifying his or her associates. If spies were played in this manner, they could be

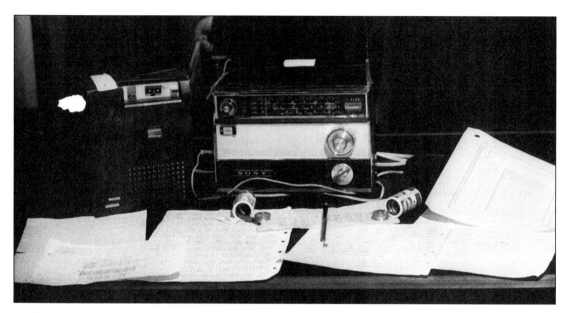

tricked into divulging even more important secrets.

In an attempt to prevent codes from being broken, intelligence agencies rushed to develop more sophisticated ciphers. At the end of World War II and the beginning of the Cold War, some of the most sophisticated were those that used not only a codebook (a book of standard codes that both the agent transmitting and the agent receiving use to encode and decode the transmission), but also a one-time pad to double-encipher information.

In this system, the codebook is used again and again, but each one-time pad is used only once. For example, to double-encipher the message "attack launched," the sender would first use the codebook to put the words into code. In so doing, the sender finds out that according to the code being used, the word "attack" will be coded

From left to right: tape recorder; code sheets; radio transmitter; hollow batteries. Devices like these allowed spies to intercept and decode radio transmissions during the Cold War.

into 4732 and the word "launched" will become 7538. Now the code itself must be put into code, or double-enciphered. Both the sender and the receiver have the same set of one-time pads and designate which one they will use. On that pad is a list of random numbers. If the first number is 1000, then the sender adds 1000 to the first coded word being sent and "4732" becomes "5732." If the second number is "1," "7538" becomes "7539." Once a pad is used, it is thrown away. At the other end, the receiver uses the one-time pad and codebook to decode the message. Author Ernest Volkman explains the beauty of this coding system:

Such ciphers, which amounted to what the cryptanalysts called "double encipherment," were virtually unbreakable, for each message was using, literally, a new cipher. Even if the cryptanalysts managed to obtain the codebook, they would still be stumped without knowing the numbers on the "one-time pad."[32]

VENONA Decrypts

VENONA was a "one-time pad" code used by the Soviets to transmit highly confidential diplomatic information and, as such, it was thought to be unbreakable. Unfortunately for the KGB, it was not and instead became one of the NSA's greatest communications intelligence achievements during the Cold War. The decrypting of VENONA actually began in 1944 in Coonawarra, Australia. It was there that a group of U.S., British, and Australian technicians monitored a radio-interception post around the clock. One day, they began to pick up Soviet transmissions.

During the Cold War a codebook like this one would be used one time and then discarded.

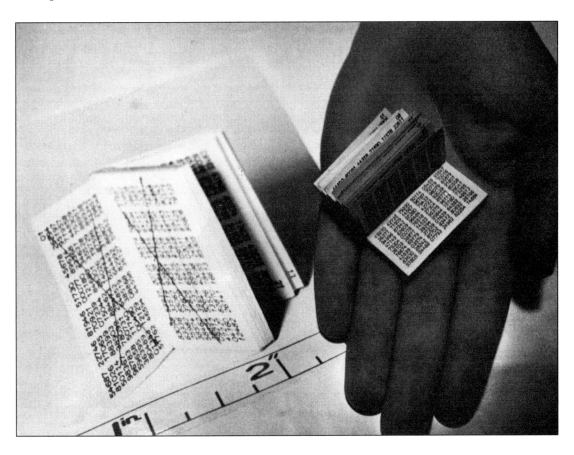

They knew immediately they were receiving encoded high-level intelligence information. They also recognized that the information was coded using the unbreakable, "one-time pad" system. Still, the technicians diligently wrote down each number they received. Their efforts were not wasted. For while the "one-time pad" system itself was unbreakable, the human beings who used it made errors. In some cases the same "pad" was used more than once; in others, code clerks had used easily breakable codes to transmit high-level information.

These little cracks in the code, in combination with information and codebooks obtained from former KGB agents such as Gouzenko, were just enough for cryptanalysts—most notably Meredith Gardner who is generally credited with the big breakthrough in decrypting VENONA in 1948—to begin to break portions of it. As parts of VENONA were decrypted, the United States learned the shocking truth of just how few of their secrets were in fact secret. As Ernest Volkman writes, "Judging by what the Russians were transmitting back to Moscow, virtually every [U.S. and British] secret was an open book."[33] This included the vigorously safeguarded top-secret Manhattan Project.

While all of the VENONA transmissions have never been decrypted, the information gleaned from those that were was very useful to the CIA. It led them to KGB agents and helped them recognize the security flaws in their systems. There was also a psychological advantage to the decrypts. Since it was impossible for the KGB to know which transmissions cryptanalysts would be able to figure out, it was impossible to know which operations and agents were safe and which were in jeopardy. Therefore, some officers and agents who would never have been identified through the decrypted information were nevertheless exfiltrated back to the USSR. For the amount of high-level information and the psychological advantage they provided, the VENONA decrypts are typically considered a huge success in communications intelligence during the Cold War.

POCHIN and PROBA

The Soviets had minimal success intercepting valuable radio signals. The 1967 KGB Annual Report raved that "as a result of decoding and deciphering [intercepted radio communications from 2,002 active stations] we read communications in 152 cipher-systems of 72 capitalist countries; in 1967 we broke 11 cipher-systems, and decoded 188,400 telegrams overall."[34] However, most of this yielded no critical information. The KGB's two most profitable radio interception programs against the United States were POCHIN and PROBA. The first POCHIN intercept post came into being in 1966. It boldly sat just a few blocks away from the White House, on the top floor of the Soviet embassy in Washington, D.C. Agents at the POCHIN station were able to listen to the nonsecure channels used by local law enforce-

Planting Bugs

In January 1998 Markus Wolf was interviewed for a CNN special called "Cold War." For roughly thirty years, Wolf was the head of the East German foreign intelligence department, the HVA, which was part of the state police, or Stasi. The following is an excerpt from this interview as it appears on the CNN website at www.cnn.com in which Wolf discusses his opinion of the value of listening devices:

> We planted bugs, microphones, in premises which interested us in the West. We weren't too successful—I would have said unfortunately in former years, but I don't care anymore now. But strangely enough, we were successful with Egon Bahr, one of the closest collaborators of [West German Chancellor] Willy Brandt, and we managed to monitor his confidential talks with an emissary from Moscow, which was interesting—and we had no information [about the talks]

from Moscow at the time—but it wasn't of decisive importance.

> Most of the results of using technical bugging devices were of little importance for my service. It may have been different in counter-intelligence, where bugs in flats, etc., were used to obtain a lot of information about what counter-intelligence was interested in. There was a lot of superfluous stuff, in my opinion, when other people were monitored: those with dissenting opinions, people in hotels, what people suspected of being spies said in hotels. . . . Of course, counter-intelligence used [technology] in [monitoring] . . . journalists, foreigners, [and other] people who were suspected [of being spies], but all in all, as far as my service, the HVA, was concerned, the use of technical means played a subordinate role.

ment, the FBI, the State Department, the Pentagon, and the White House. As time went on and POCHIN successfully intercepted these communications, four other POCHIN intercept sites were established in the Washington, D.C., metro area.

The success of POCHIN in monitoring the goings-on in Washington led the KGB to begin monitoring another key U.S. city, New York. They code-named this program PROBA, and its development was similar to that of POCHIN. It began with one radio intercept post in the Soviet residency in New York City, and eventually came to include four intercept stations in and around the New York City area. Although PROBA and POCHIN were con-

cerned primarily with listening in on non-secure conversations in the cities of New York and Washington, they nevertheless yielded results. The Soviets found some of the information quite valuable. Authors Christopher Andrew and Vasili Mitrokhin give "secret data on the vetting of ninety candidates for posts in the first Nixon administration"[35] as an example of the type of valuable information these intercept posts provided.

Operation Gold

Communications intelligence can also involve intercepting communications passed along a wire, such as telephone conversations. This is called "tapping" the wire. In order to intercept these messages, the intelligence organization must have physical access to the wire they wish to tap. Therefore, since an agent must get to the wire to tap it, as was the case with bugging an important room, there is a degree of risk associated with wiretapping.

One of the most interesting wiretaps occurred in the German city of Berlin. Following World War II, Berlin was divided into four zones—the U.S. zone, the British zone, the French zone, and the Soviet zone. As time went on, the U.S., British, and French zones were merged to form West Berlin, which was part of West Germany, and the Soviet sector became East Berlin, which was part of East Germany. In this divided city the United States and the Soviets held positions just a few hundred feet away from each other, and the CIA undertook Operation Gold.

Operation Gold was part of an epic battle in communications intelligence. After VENONA was exposed, the Soviets found a new way to send radio messages at an ultrahigh frequency that could not be intercepted. Suddenly, the Western nations could no longer listen in on Soviet conversations and the Soviets seemed to

Tapping a telephone. The CIA's Operation Gold involved tapping Soviet telephone lines in Berlin in the mid-1950s.

Operation Gold

The following short article appeared in *Life* magazine on May 7, 1956, and detailed the Soviet "discovery" of Operation Gold.

Last week in Berlin the Russians were smiling with righteous indignation. Ten feet below ground, next to a cemetery in their own sector, they uncovered a tunnel which led into the U.S. sector of Berlin. The pumps and ventilating equipment in it all had U.S. labels, proof, the Russians cried, that it had been dug by the U.S. to spy on them. They led newsmen to a room crammed with British-made wire-tapping apparatus and a tape recorder. The [wiretaps] were fastened to three underground cables, two belonging to the East German government and one used by the Red army, presumably to connect Berlin headquarters with Moscow.

When they weren't complaining, the Russians were full of frank respect for whoever had installed such a set-up right under their noses. They thought the tapping had begun in 1954 when U.S. forces constructed a small radar station near the East Berlin border which, the Russians implied, had been set up largely as cover for the wire-tapping.

U.S. officials in Berlin dismissed Russian spy charges as "ridiculous." But West Berliners, who sometimes feel the U.S. shows too little initiative in its cold war with the Reds, were proud and delighted. They guessed the U.S. must have overheard a lot in the two years the tunnel lay hidden. Said one West Berlin cop to an American friend: "It's a pity they found it but I hope you have some spares."

have the upper hand in intelligence collection once again. In Berlin the CIA worked with the SIS to counter this by tapping the Russian telephone lines. However, the KGB was already one step ahead of them. Recognizing what their rival intelligence agencies were doing, the Soviets began scrambling their phone lines to make it impossible for the CIA and SIS to glean any information from their phone taps. Luckily for the CIA, a top-notch signals intelligence officer, Carl Nelson, was on their side. Nathan Miller explains that Nelson "discovered that a trace of the actual voice transmission remained on a telephone line for a split second after being scrambled and that this 'shadow' could be picked up."[36]

On the heels of this discovery, the CIA also learned that the landlines carrying communications from the Soviet military and intelligence headquarters in East Berlin lay six feet underground and roughly five hundred meters away from the part of Berlin occupied by the United States. They could tap these lines if only they could reach them, and thus Operation Gold was born. It was a joint project undertaken by the CIA, the British SIS, and the West German intelligence agency. Working together, they devised and implemented a plan to tunnel five hundred meters underground from the U.S. sector to the Soviet sector in order to tap the phone lines. Since the soil was loose and they had to tunnel right underneath the heavily guarded border, U.S. Army engineers worked many long hours burrowing only a few feet at a time to avoid cave-ins and prevent the border guards above from noticing. On February 22, 1955, Operation Gold succeeded in reaching and tapping the phone lines.

However, Soviet spies were one step ahead and knew about the plans for the tunnel before its construction had even begun. Way back in 1954 a KGB officer named George Blake (whom the Soviets had recruited soon after the Magnificent Five were exposed) had given his controller a copy of the CIA–SIS plans to build a tunnel. However, the KGB did not want to compromise their agent by acknowledging they knew of the tunnel so they let the CIA–SIS collect information for roughly a year and found ways to protect their own important communiqués. The CIA–SIS was still able to glean important information. Christopher Andrew and Vasili Mitrokhin write that the CIA–SIS learned about

> important new information on the improved nuclear capability of the Soviet air force in East Germany; its new fleet of bombers and twin-jet radar-equipped interceptors; the doubling of Soviet bomber strength and the creation of a new fighter division in Poland; over one hundred air force installations in the USSR, GDR and Poland; the organization, bases and personnel of the Soviet Baltic Fleet;

and installations and personnel of the Soviet atomic energy program.[37]

In fact, Operation Gold yielded so much information that it took until September 1958, nearly two and a half years after the tunnel was "discovered" and sealed, to finish processing the information gathered. As for the KGB's discovery of the tunnel, it was a well-planned media event. On April 25, 1956, reporters from West Berlin received a rare invitation to East Berlin for a press conference. At the conference the Soviets claimed that they had discovered the existence of the tun-

KGB officer George Blake gathered intelligence that led to the exposure of Operation Gold in 1956.

nel four days earlier. This tunnel, they told reporters, was built to intercept military communications, and was, therefore, criminal espionage. Then, to cap the event, the reporters were taken on a tour of the tunnel itself.

Of course, now it is obvious that the KGB did not discover the tunnel in April 1956, but instead knew of it from its inception in 1954. All along the KGB was aware of the fact that their communications were being listened to, but in light of the information collected they do not appear to have taken steps to safeguard all Soviet high-level information by warning the GRU or the military. As a result, the United States and Great Britain were able to collect a great deal of data on the Soviet armed forces. The final twist to the Operation Gold story is that the information collected revealed there was a Soviet mole working inside the SIS. Five years later, with the help of a KGB agent who defected to the West, that mole was identified as Blake.

As the Cold War progressed, communications operations evolved and became more important (and useful) in the battle. In combination with other types of technical intelligence collection, such as aerial reconnaissance, the CIA was able to rely on superior technology to gather information on the Soviet Union. The Soviets had been able to gather this sort of information in the United States for years through case officers and agents, but technology allowed the United States to even the score.

Chapter 5

Active Measures and Covert Operations

As the Cold War progressed, some case officers and agents were asked to perform tasks designed to directly influence the behavior of other governments. In the KGB these were called "active measures" or "special tasks," while the CIA called them "covert operations." These tasks ranged from spreading propaganda and finding targets for sabotage to extensive paramilitary operations. In a war between two superpowers that never actually fired directly at each other, these operations were where battles were won and lost, and the intelligence officer was the soldier.

Covert Operations

Covert action is a term used in the United States to refer to a specific type of task undertaken by the CIA. What distinguishes these tasks from others performed by the CIA is their goal. Whereas the majority of work done by the agency is carried out in an attempt to collect in-formation, the goal of covert action is to achieve a foreign policy objective. In other words, it is not just observing the government of another country; it is actively working to get that country to do what is in the United States' best interest, and, as the word covert implies, it is doing so secretly. During the Cold War, the secretive nature of some operations was especially necessary in instances where the U.S. government needed to be able to deny knowledge of an operation. The American intelligence community calls this "plausible deniability."

While the United States was the only nation that used the phrase "covert action," it was not alone in its use of such operations during the Cold War. The Soviets also engaged in such activities, which they called "active measures" (*ak-tivnye meropriiatiia*), in the hope that they could influence a given country to behave in the USSR's best interests. The Soviet term differs a bit from covert action because it includes all "overt and covert techniques of influencing events and behavior in, and the actions of, foreign countries."[38] In other words, covert action has to be secret, but active measures can be done out in the open or in secret.

A Soviet WWII propaganda poster. Spreading propaganda was practiced by both superpowers during the Cold War.

ВСЁ ДЛЯ ФРОНТА!

ДАДИМ КРАСНОЙ АРМИИ БОЛЬШЕ
ТАНКОВ, САМОЛЕТОВ, ОРУДИЙ, ПУЛЕМЕТОВ
ВИНТОВОК, СНАРЯДОВ, ПАТРОНОВ!

As the Cold War escalated, covert action and active measures came to include a variety of operations, some of which were violent and bloody, others that appear to be crackpot schemes in retrospect. Operations could be directed at either a friendly government or an adversary. Within the country, they could target government officials in power, political groups who were not in power, or the populace at large. The most widely known covert operations were attempts by the Soviets or the United States either to help a political group seize control in a given country or assassinate foreign leaders. However, there were many other types of covert action employed in the Cold War, including sabotage and propaganda.

Active Measures in Eastern Europe

The most infamous active measures undertaken by the KGB came at the beginning of the Cold War, and some would argue, started it. In the wake of World War II, many war torn countries were left with no functioning government. Both the United States and the Soviets saw these nations without governments as an opportunity to get more allies on their respective Cold War teams. The United States hoped countries would choose to be democratic or at least have governments that were friendly to U.S. foreign policy goals. Meanwhile, the Soviet leader, Joseph Stalin, saw this as an opportunity to create a buffer zone of Communist states friendly to Russia.

Stalin did not simply hope that these countries would become Communist, he ordered the KGB to take active measures to ensure that they did. These active measures focused on providing support—financial and military—to groups friendly to the Soviets and fostering their violent coups to take over Eastern European nations. In this way, as historian Christopher Andrew explains, "people's democracies," a term used to refer to Communist systems that were loyal to Moscow, "were imposed on the countries of Eastern Europe by a combination of force and deception, in which the [KGB] played a central role."[39]

Joseph Stalin led the Soviet expansion into Eastern Europe following WWII.

The Communist Takeover of Poland

The KGB (called the NKVD at the time) used a variety of tactics to ensure Communist regimes loyal to Moscow were installed in Eastern Europe. Active measures were deployed in 1941 in Poland, where the first step was to find, or create, a Communist political group friendly to the Soviets. The Polish Communist Party had ceased to exist in 1938, so in 1941 Stalin decided to revive it for his purposes. He called on the KGB to do so. In December a group of KGB officers parachuted into Poland and worked to reestablish contact with the prewar leaders of the Polish Communist Party. They found former leader Wladyslaw Gomulka and named him secretary of the newly revived Warsaw Party. Over the next few years, the KGB worked with the local Communists to build up a following and a militia.

The second phase of Soviet takeover was the creation of a somewhat legitimate coalition government that included Communists as well as members of other non-Communist Polish political groups such as the Home Army. In 1944, when the Soviets were certain the new Communist party had a decent following in Poland, Stalin established the Polish National Committee of Liberation in Lublin (frequently called the Lublin Committee, named after the Polish city).

The next step in the takeover was to eliminate all other groups that might op-

Wladyslaw Gomulka was appointed secretary of the Polish Warsaw Party by the KGB in 1941.

the Nazis and the Home Army over the next two months while the Russian Army sat nearby watching, but did not help. In the end, the Nazis crushed the Home Army insurrection but were themselves greatly weakened. It was then that the Russian Army came in and defeated the Nazis.

Once they took over Warsaw, the Soviets put the KGB back to work ferreting out any remaining Home Army supporters and killing them. The KGB made certain any leaders of the Home Army that might have challenged a Communist-controlled government were eliminated, leaving the path clear for Stalin to declare the government the one and only Communist government of Poland. With the opposition out of the way, in early 1945 the Lublin Committee declared itself the provisional government of Poland, and the USSR formally recognized it as such. The Soviets had achieved their foreign policy goals, in part, through the active measures of the KGB.

However, these measures were not covert, and foreign governments could see the hand of the KGB in bringing the Lublin government into power. Believing the people of Poland did not control their new government, the United States refused to recognize it as legitimate. In order to "prove" to the rest of the world that the Polish people did support the new Lublin regime, in 1945 the Soviets told the United States they would hold an election. Thus began the next phase of

pose Communist leadership in both the Lublin government and Poland. This was accomplished through deception as the Soviets cleverly pitted their enemies against each other so that each would be weakened. For instance, as the Russian Army moved toward Warsaw, a Soviet radio broadcast encouraged the Home Army, a non-Communist resistance movement in Poland, to arms, urging them to rise up and fight the German occupying forces, the Nazis. More than 250,000 Polish people died in the fighting between the takeover—ensuring that the Lublin government won the election.

Rigged Elections

In the case of Poland, these elections had to be delayed until 1947 because the Polish version of the KGB, which was called the UB and operated under the control of KGB advisers, had to learn how to properly rig the election (this involved stuffing ballot boxes, and bribing and intimidating voters). In the end, the Lublin government won, but it was still obvious the KGB-led UB rigged the elections. Regardless, the Lublin government was firmly entrenched in power. The UB and the KGB eliminated any opposition that

arose, and soon after the rigged elections, all other parties were abolished. The only choice in the next election would be the candidates that Moscow supported. Since their campaign in Poland was successful, the Soviets used this blueprint for the takeover of other Eastern European nations such as East Germany, Rumania, Bulgaria, Hungary, and Czechoslovakia.

The CIA Influences Italian Elections

As Russia shored up its western borders and country after country became Communist, the United States and its Western European allies became progressively nervous. When Czechoslovakia came under

Influencing the Italian Elections

In his book, *The CIA Under Reagan, Bush & Casey: The Evolution of the Agency from Roosevelt to Reagan,* former deputy director of the CIA, Dr. Ray S. Cline, explains the U.S. motivation to intervene in the Italian elections from his perspective.

> With respect to Italy in particular, which had an election scheduled for April 1948, Americans with knowledge of Italy, especially Americans with family connections or religious ties to the Catholic hierarchy, were sought to carry a message to Italian voters that association with the United States would save Italy whereas Communist rule would destroy it. The methods employed were psychological and political. Mainly they involved teaching American electoral techniques . . . and providing money for local political groups to organize, counter Communist propaganda, and get out the vote. . . .

The weakest point in Western Europe in the bleak winter of 1947–1948 was undoubtedly Italy. . . . [Top-secret National Security Council, or NSC] papers show that it was very much feared that the Communist Party of Italy would defeat the moderate, center, and right parties that supported parliamentary government and a Western strategic alignment. . . . Key passages from the conclusion of the NSC [about how to handle the situation] read:

The United States should make full use of its political, economic and if necessary, military power in such a manner as may be found most effective to assist in preventing Italy from falling under the domination of the USSR either through external armed attack or through Soviet-dominated Communist movements within Italy. . . .

Communist control in early 1948, the United States worried the Soviets might also take over parts of Western Europe. In an attempt to ensure this did not happen, the United States resorted to covert actions. The Communist parties in France and Italy were the two largest in Western Europe. After Czechoslovakia became Communist, the French and Italian parties appeared all the more threatening to the United States. The Italian parliamentary elections were fast approaching, and it looked as though the Communists could become the ruling party in the Italian government through democratic elections. Fearing this would be a first step toward Soviet expansion into Italy, President Truman acted to ensure that Communists would not win the election.

Similar to the plan of the Soviets, Truman wanted to provide support to groups that would be friendly to his government if they came to power. The goal was clear—stop the Communists from winning control of the Italian government in the upcoming election. For the United States this meant supporting non-Communist political organizations in Italy. Truman knew this aid must be given to these organizations covertly because if the Italian people knew they were receiving U.S. aid, the organizations would be seen as false and no one would vote for them.

Truman called on the newly founded CIA to keep the Italian Communist Party from winning the majority in Italy. They accomplished this primarily through fi-

nancial means; in the end, between $10 million and $30 million was spent keeping the Communists out of power. This money was used to finance the campaigns of non-Communist politicians and also to construct a propaganda campaign against their Communist opponents. The propaganda was designed to frighten Italian voters, attempting to convince them that voting for the Communists would lead directly to a Soviet takeover.

In addition, the CIA also asked tens of thousands of Italian Americans to write letters to their families in Italy pleading with them not to vote for the Communists. The CIA was also able to convince some Vatican officials to speak out against Communist candidates. Since Italy was home to a number of Catholics who looked to the Vatican for guidance on political matters, this had a significant influence. On election day, CIA officers even bribed election officials in certain districts within Italy to make sure a non-Communist candidate won. When the results were tallied, the CIA's covert operation was a success. The election came and went with the Christian Democrats winning 307 of 574 seats in the Italian Parliament, and thus controlling the government.

Proxies

The takeover of Eastern Europe and the influencing of the Italian elections represent one type of covert action—a country influencing the affairs of a foreign nation by supporting a political group within that nation that is friendly to its goals. For the Soviets in Poland this meant military and financial support, for the United States in Italy it was limited to financial support, propaganda, and the use of intelligence personnel.

The United States and the Soviets also used their intelligence agencies to support other, more violent groups within nations throughout the Cold War. Since it was politically dangerous for either the CIA or the KGB actually to be associated with the overthrowing of governments and leaders, they increasingly turned to supporting terrorist groups, or proxies, that would carry out these tasks. The intelligence agencies arranged arms shipments, provided strategic planning, paramilitary training, and money to a variety of these groups around the world.

In the late 1960s and early 1970s the KGB used a number of terrorist proxies. It shipped arms to the Irish Republican Army (IRA) to aid in its fight against British troops. It also provided weapons to the anti-Israeli group, the Popular Front for the Liberation of Palestine, which received a significant arms shipment in exchange for abducting a CIA officer. Finally, the KGB threw its support behind the Sandinista National Libera-

Troops from the Popular Front for the Liberation of Palestine brandish automatic weapons in 1966. The anti-Israeli organization was one of several KGB proxies established in the late 1960s.

Plotting Assasination

Vasili Mitrokhin's files from Christopher Andrew and Vasili Mitrokhin, *The Sword and the Shield: The Mitrokhin Archive and the Secret History of the KGB* contained information on the planning of Marshall Tito's assassination. The KGB assassin who volunteered to shoot Tito, Iosif Grigulevich, offered up the following four possible ways to eliminate him:

1. To administer a lethal dose of pneumonic plague from a silent spray concealed in his [Grigulevich's] clothing during a personal audience with Tito. (Grigulevich would be inoculated with an antidote beforehand.)

2. To obtain an invitation to the reception for Tito to be given during his forthcoming visit to London by the Yugoslav ambassador, with whom Grigulevich was on friendly terms. Grigulevich would shoot Tito with a silenced pistol, then spray tear gas at the reception to cause panic and make his escape.

3. To use the previous method at a diplomatic reception in Belgrade.

4. To present Tito with jewelry in a booby-trapped box which would release a lethal poison gas as soon as it was opened.

tion Front in Nicaragua, which was engaged in some sabotage activities in the United States. Later on in the Cold War the United States supported the Contras in Nicaragua who worked against the Sandinistas.

Assassination

Another type of covert action was the elimination of a powerful group or individual that posed a problem in a foreign country. During the Cold War the United States and the Soviet Union each attempted to use assassination to deal with individuals and groups found to be threatening to their national security or economic interests. While the Soviets were successful in some attempts, the United States was not.

In the early years of the Cold War, assassination of inconvenient leaders was a very important part of the foreign policy of both superpowers. In U.S. intelligence lingo this was referred to as "executive action." A number of world leaders were marked for executive action in the early 1960s. Poisoning was typically the method of choice and Dr. Stanley Gottlieb, the head of the Technical Services Staff and an expert on toxins, cooked up some nasty potions for agency use.

Patrice Lumumba, a Congolese premier, was an early target. The CIA was set to poison him; two vials of Dr. Gottlieb's toxic concoction had already arrived at the CIA station in the Congo. However, Lumumba was ousted and killed by opposition groups within the Congo (the degree of CIA complicity remains in dispute) before he could be poisoned. Iraqi leader Colonel Kassem was also earmarked for executive action, but killed by other forces before the CIA could assassinate him. Miller explains that "a handkerchief impregnated with a toxic substance was sent to him through the mail. Before it arrived, the intended victim [Kassem] had already been overthrown and shot."[40]

However, the main target of the CIA's assassination attempts and schemes was the Cuban dictator, Fidel Castro. Since Castro always smoked cigars, they toyed with the idea of dipping cigars in a poison so toxic it would kill him upon his first puff. In the end, they decided to enlist the help of the Mafia, which had a vested interest in getting rid of Castro—he had shut down their gambling, drug, and prostitution businesses in Cuba when he assumed power. The CIA met with John Rosselli and Sam "Momo" Giancana to arrange a "hit" in exchange for $150,000 and, of course, the government would then be in their debt. According to Miller, arrangements were made for a contract killer to put some of Gottlieb's poison capsules into Castro's food or beverages. They tried twice and failed.

The CIA was by no means the only intelligence agency botching assassination attempts. Assassination was an important part of Soviet foreign policy, and, as was the case with the Americans, it seldom went to plan. An early Cold War target was Marshall Tito, the Yugoslavian Communist leader who was too uppity for Stalin's liking. When Tito tried to form a Balkan federation, which Stalin saw as a threat to his power, Stalin said, "I shall shake my little finger . . . and there will be no more Tito."[41] When his attempts to dis-

credit and unseat Tito failed, Stalin told the KGB (then called the MGB) to assassinate Tito. However, Stalin died before the plan could come to fruition and his successor, Nikita Khrushchev, suspended those plans.

The KGB was successful, however, in the murder of the president of Afghanistan, Hafizullah Amin. Believing that Amin was going to end Communist rule in Afghanistan, KGB chairman, Yuri Andropov, decided he

Cuban dictator Fidel Castro puffs a cigar in 1962. On a number of occasions the CIA attempted to assassinate Castro. However, all attempts failed.

must be assassinated. On December 27, 1979, Amin was gunned down when seven hundred KGB officers disguised in Afghan military uniforms stormed the presidential palace.

Propaganda

Not all covert action is undertaken on such as large a scale or is as violent as assassination. Sometimes simple propaganda is used to influence the affairs of another nation. Propaganda is either information or misinformation that is consistently and methodically spread among the citizens of a country to promote or injure a cause. It is frequently part of larger campaigns by intelligence organizations.

This was the case in the 1954 CIA-assisted ousting of Guatemala's first democratically elected president, Jacobo Arbenz. To stir up anti-Arbenz sentiments among the public, the CIA covertly set up a fake radio station, called the Voice of Liberation, in a neighboring country. It pretended to be a rebel, clandestine station broadcasting from inside Guatemala, and its purpose was to disseminate propaganda to induce Guatemalan citizens to support the CIA's choice, Carlos Castillo Armas, in overthrowing Arbenz.

Roughly six weeks before Armas planned to march his troops into Guatemala City and forcibly take over the government, the CIA station went on the air. David Atlee Phillips, the CIA officer who acted as an adviser to the radio team, explains the station's goals:

Carlos Castillo Armas assumed leadership of Guatemala in 1954, following a CIA supported coup.

By [the scheduled day of attack] the Voice of Liberation had to create the proper psychological climate for rebellion and transform part of the listening audience into activists. To do this the basic premises of the rebel movement were defined in the initial broadcasts. Next, special programs were designed to influence specific groups. The women announcers exhorted Guatemalan women to sway their husbands and sons. Soldiers were told why their duty lay with the rebels rather than with those who would sell out the country to foreigners. Workers were wooed, youth was cajoled. There was a revolutionary something for everyone. Decision time was drawing near! Would the listener be with the winners or the losers.[42]

The Voice of Liberation's attempts to create a hostile climate for Arbenz and a welcoming one for Armas were successful. The station even played a role in the final victory by broadcasting misinformation that large numbers of Armas's troops, which did not actually exist in any formidable number, were advancing and approaching the capital. Arbenz resigned and Armas was accepted as the new Guatemalan leader, in part as the result of a very successful propaganda campaign.

Thus, throughout the Cold War the CIA and the KGB used active measures and covert operations to influence the governments or populace of other nations. Whether it was using propaganda to convince a group of people to revolt, rigging elections, or using more violent means such as assassination and the support of proxies, the end goal was the same. Each agency was attempting to ensure that the government of a given nation acted in the best interests of the agency's country. Most of the time, this was done without ever having to use overtly military means. However, there were instances in the Cold War where military intervention was used, and the conflict between the superpowers became more heated.

Chapter 6

The Cold War Heats Up

Much of the Cold War featured rhetoric and fear. Soviet leaders would denounce the United States, and the United States would return the favor. The CIA and the KGB would sneak around stealing each other's technology and government secrets while trying to infiltrate each other's agency. There was a great deal of posturing and even more paranoia about the other superpower's plan for an attack. And while an actual attack never came to pass, there were points at which the Cold War heated up. These were times when one or both of the superpowers resorted to military solutions to achieve the outcome they wanted in the world. During these times the rest of the world sat in patient fear of two countries capable of mass destruction that could devastate the globe. In this atmosphere the opponents in the Cold War found themselves marshalling military forces, training paramilitary troops, and fighting secret military battles to stop the spread of the other's ideology or protect their own interests around the globe.

The KGB and the Korean War

The first heated situation came in Korea. At the end of World War II, Korea was divided into northern and southern occupation zones separated by a longitudinal line called the 38th parallel. In 1948 the Soviets formally recognized the Communist People's Democratic Republic as the government of North Korea, while the United States backed the Republic of South Korea. When both superpowers withdrew from the divided country in 1949, the North and South Koreans were left to resolve their reunification problems by themselves.

On June 25, 1950, the North Koreans decided to resolve the issue by invading South Korea, Kim Il-Sung, the Communist dictator of North Korea, traveled to Moscow weeks before the invasion to secure Stalin's support. The invasion had

Stalin's blessing. President Truman, in turn, feared a Communist takeover of South Korea was part of a massive plan on the part of Stalin for Soviet expansion around the world and opposed it. Without hesitation he sent U.S. troops to defend South Korea.

Although Stalin politically supported Kim Il-Sung's invasion, be never committed Soviet military forces to the war. However, since Moscow's sympathies lay with the North Koreans, KGB officers and agents worked to provide information on the war for the North Koreans. Fortunately for Kim Il-Sung's troops, the KGB was in an excellent position to gather this political and military information. Two members of the Magnificent Five, Kim Philby and Donald Maclean, held powerful positions in Washington that allowed them access to a great deal of sensitive information about the war.

This rare photograph shows KGB spy Donald Maclean (far right) in action during his employment as First Secretary for the British Embassy in Washington, D.C., in 1951.

And report the two men did. They gave Moscow numerous classified documents about U.S. military decisions, intentions, and the war, which the KGB then turned over to the North Koreans. In retrospect, Maclean's deputy Robert Cecil concluded the documents Maclean had access to would have been "of inestimable value in advising the . . . North Koreans on strategy and negotiating positions."[43]

The CIA and the Korean War

While the KGB supplied the North Koreans with invaluable information, their American counterparts had difficulty collecting first-rate intelligence and analyzing it. Despite significant troop buildups prior to the invasion, the CIA had failed to anticipate that Kim Il-Sung would invade the south. Similarly, shortly after the war began, U.S. forces drove the invaders back across the 38th parallel and needed the CIA to ascertain whether the Chinese Communists would attack if U.S. forces were to cross the 38th parallel and attempt to take over North Korea. "While full-scale Chinese Communist intervention must be regarded as a possibility," the agency concluded, "barring a Soviet decision for global war, such action is not probable in 1950."[44] They were wrong, and crossing the 38th parallel not only brought the Chinese Communists into the war, it drove the U.S. forces back into South Korea.

CIA covert operations did not fare much better, although they had a few successes. For instance, roughly half a dozen

North Korean leader Kim Il-Sung in 1950. That same year Il-Sung invaded South Korea.

operatives successfully infiltrated the Soviet naval base at Vladivostok. From this vantage point they could alert the United States if the Soviets decided to enter the war. CIA officers also managed to sever the cable the Chinese Communists used for troop communications. This, in turn, forced the Chinese to use radio transmissions to communicate, which then could be intercepted.

Operation Stole was another victory for the CIA. The Chinese Communists were facing a medical epidemic; a significant number of their troops were stricken with illness. As a neutral nation, India agreed to provide humanitarian aid to the Chinese and sent medical supplies and field hospitals for use in battling the plague. The CIA intervened to keep the medical supplies from reaching the troops. They made arrangements with the Chinese Nationalists (enemies of the Chinese Communists) and the medical supply ship was stopped on the high seas and pirated so that the cargo never reached the ailing troops. While it appeared to be the work of China Sea pirates or the Chinese Nationalists, in reality, it was the CIA that masterminded the operation.

In addition to these covert actions that dealt with intelligence gathering and sabotage, the CIA organized a covert military operation. They recruited and trained more than a thousand Koreans in combat techniques at a facility on Yong-do Island. These new troops, called paramilitary troops because they fought either in place of or to supplement the U.S. military troops, eventually began making commando raids for the CIA and gathering intelligence for use in battle.

While the Korean War ended in a standoff with neither side truly victorious, the CIA could claim victory despite the minimal success of its operations. Due to the expectations placed on the CIA to deploy covert action operations for the war, this section of the organization, called the Operation of Policy Coordination (OPC), had expanded significantly. Not only had operating

Anticipating an Invasion

The National Security Agency's website at www.nsa.org contains a history of cryptology in the Korean War. The following excerpt explains that there were relatively few communications intercepted through communications intelligence [COMINT] that could have given the United States advance warning of the North Korean invasion of South Korea.

As it happened, prior to 1950 there were two COMINT hints [that the North Koreans would invade the South], but neither was sufficient to provide specific warning of a June invasion. In the spring of 1950, a Soviet network in the Vladivostok area greatly increased its targeting of communications in South Korea. Soviet targeting of South Korea was quite low until early February, then rose dramatically after the 21st. This coverage continued at a very high level until 15 May, when it ceased altogether.

In the second case, as revealed in COMINT, large shipments of bandages and medicines went from the USSR to North Korea and Manchuria, starting in February 1950.

These two actions made sense only in hindsight, after the invasion of South Korea occurred in June 1950.

COMINT, supported by information from other open and secret sources, showed a number of other military-related activities, such as VIP visits and communications changes, in the Soviet Far East and in the PRC, but none was suspicious in itself. Even when consolidated by AFSA in early 1951, these activities as a whole did not provide clear evidence that . . . a North Korean invasion of the South [was imminent].

procedures and the organizational structure been created, it had also taken on a military role in the war, and the CIA officers with it. These established covert forces would become the backbone of other CIA operations throughout the Cold War.

The Bay of Pigs Invasion

January 2, 1959, marked the beginning of the next hot spot in the Cold War. On this day, the Twenty-Sixth of July Movement led by Fidel Castro succeeded in overthrowing the Batista dictatorship in Cuba, and Castro seized power. At this time Castro was not a Communist nor was his party a Communist party. However, as time went on he nationalized the land in Cuba, which means the land belonged to Cuba (the nation) instead of individual landowners. This structure of land ownership is a fundamental part of communism, and therefore the United States grew wary. Also, while he appealed to both the United States and the Soviets for aid to complete his revolution, it was the USSR who supported him. To assist and woo Castro, the KGB sent well over a hundred advisers to shore up his intelligence and security systems. Less than a year later the Soviet Union formally recognized Castro's regime as the government of Cuba.

The friendliness that was developing between the Soviets and Cuba frightened the United States because it meant the Soviets now had an ally on the U.S. side of the globe, and one in their own backyard to boot. The United States had always had allies geographically close to the Soviet Union and was, therefore, able to place nuclear warheads, that could easily reach the Soviets, in Western European states such as Great Britain and Turkey. Now the United States worried that if the Castro regime aligned with Moscow, the Soviets would be able to place nuclear warheads in Cuba.

After CIA-led assassination attempts failed, the organization began working to remove Castro from power in a plan called "Operation Pluto." The goal was first to locate a rebel leader who, once in power, would see eye to eye with the United States, then to assist him in mounting a paramilitary attack to seize power in Cuba—or, in reality, mount that invasion for him.

Thus, to overthrow Castro the CIA concluded they would need to find a rebel group, train thousands of exiles as a ground force for it, fashion an air force and a navy to support the ground forces, and all the while make it appear as though this was all done by an anti-Castro group. In addition, the U.S. hand in the operation could not be seen so that the president could believably deny any American involvement.

The CIA started small, setting up a radio station as they had done in Guatemala, but this time, to send anti-Castro programming across the airwaves. Then, the search for a fitting rebel leader began. This proved quite difficult since Castro

Masking U.S. Involvement in the Bay of Pigs

In the following excerpt from *The Night Watch*, David Atlee Phillips discusses one propaganda campaign that he headed up for the CIA as part of the Bay of Pigs invasion in an effort to maintain plausible deniability for President Kennedy.

Four days before the invasion. The first strike was scheduled for April 15, D-Day minus two. Abruptly, I became involved in the air action. As another of the last minute efforts to mask United States involvement, and to make the external aspects of the exile attack appear to be "internal," it was decided the first strike must seem to originate in Cuba. Three Cuban airfields were to be bombarded, but in a manner which would make it appear that defecting Castro pilots had done it, rather than exile planes from Central America. It was my assignment during the next twenty-four hours to stage-manage the incredible charade. . . .

I worked desperately to work out the scenario to be followed by the "defecting" pilots and crews; one plane was to land in Key West, another in Miami. They would claim to airport authorities—and to American newsmen—that they had attacked Castro's aircraft after a decision to defect with their planes. . . . I sent a series of cables to the airbase in Nicaragua so that the crews selected for the deception would be prepared: what they should wear, what they should say, and that at least minor damage should be done to the aircraft before take-

President Kennedy failed to maintain plausible deniability throughout the Bay of Pigs invasion.

off to create the illusion that they had been in combat. . . .

[Following the actual strikes] The two exile B-26 planes carrying flying actors landed in Key West and Miami, their wild claims made more credible as a bona fide defector had landed just previously in Tampa with his Cuban plane.

had wiped out most of his opponents after seizing power. In the absence of a legitimate existing group, the CIA formulated one. Eventually they were able to align five exiled Cuban leaders to form the Cuban Democratic Revolutionary Front (FRD, or *Frente Revolucionario Democratico*) and began training their followers at Camp Trax, a base in Guatemala. The recruits were given weapons, taught how to use them, and trained in paramilitary action. Soon an air base was set up and equipped with nearly thirty U.S. planes. As for the rebel navy, the CIA acquired a fledgling company in the Florida Keys and with it two World War II vessels that would be used to land rebel troops in Cuba.

Despite the elaborate planning behind Operation Pluto, the invasion was a complete disaster. While the CIA had successfully assembled forces, it had not provided good intelligence reports, especially about the capabilities of Castro's forces. When the CIA's twelve hundred exiled Cubans tried to set up a beachhead in the Bay of Pigs on April 17, 1961, Castro anticipated the assault and defeated the rebel forces in less than three days. President Kennedy, who had taken office and given the go-ahead for the in-

vasion, was humiliated. The CIA, which had not provided either a workable plan or good intelligence, was disgraced. And Castro, who had previously approached both the United States and the USSR for assistance and alliance, was driven into the hands of the Soviets who were only too happy to have the opportunity to have an ally just off the U.S. coast.

The Cuban Missile Crisis

The Soviets quickly took advantage of this situation. Through aerial reconnaissance, the CIA knew military equipment

The body of a soldier killed during the Bay of Pigs invasion. The botched invasion opened the door for Soviet expansion into Cuba.

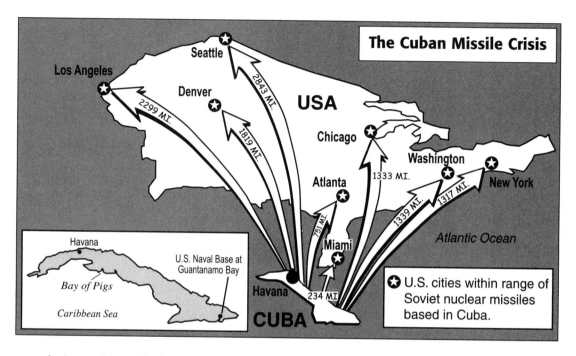

The Cuban Missile Crisis

Seattle
Los Angeles
Denver
2299 MI.
1819 MI.
2843 MI.
USA
Chicago
Atlanta
Washington
1333 MI.
New York
751 MI.
Miami
1339 MI.
1317 MI.
Atlantic Ocean
Havana
234 MI.
CUBA

Havana
U.S. Naval Base at
Guantanamo Bay
Bay of Pigs
Caribbean Sea

✪ U.S. cities within range of Soviet nuclear missiles based in Cuba.

was being shipped from the Soviet Union to Cuba throughout the summer of 1962. Their photos showed MIG jets in Cuban airfields, the arrival of Russian troops, and electronics equipment. Unfortunately for the CIA, aside from aerial reconnaissance, they had no other way to keep tabs on Cuba, and it was difficult to discern the contents of the cargo of some of the vessels.

Weapons were arriving in crates, and even U-2 spy planes could not see inside. The CIA used "crate-ology" to try to determine the contents of most of these mystery crates. According to Marchetti and Marks, crate-ology was a "unique method of determining the contents of the large crates carried on the decks of the Soviet ships delivering arms. With a

high degree of accuracy, the specialists could look at photographs of these boxes, factor in information about the ship's embarkation point and Soviet military production schedules, and deduce whether the crates contained transport aircraft or jet fighters."[45] However, despite their knowledge, there were some crates the CIA simply could not identify.

As the CIA began to hear stories from Cuban refugees about Russian rockets on flatbed trucks, it became increasingly more suspicious about the mystery crates. Based on these suspicions, U-2s took to the skies over Cuba to keep an eye on the situation (in this case operated by highly skilled U.S. Air Force pilots since Soviet SAMs made it too dangerous for CIA pilots). What they found on October 14, 1962, was photographic evidence of Soviet medium range nuclear missiles in Cuba. "With ranges up to 2,200 miles," writes Nathan Miller, "the missiles could reach targets in a large area of the United States."[46]

Over the course of the next fourteen days, President Kennedy and Soviet premier Nikita Khrushchev stared each other down over the presence of missiles in Cuba. The incident came to be known as the Cuban Missile Crisis. Khrushchev insisted Kennedy was lying about the presence of nuclear warheads in Cuba, and Kennedy argued he had photographic evidence, which was dramatically unveiled in front of United Nations delegates by Ambassador Adlai Stevenson. In the end,

Khrushchev blinked first and agreed to remove the medium-range nuclear missiles from Cuba. Throughout the fourteen days of the Cuban Missile Crisis the two superpowers faced off on the brink of all-out nuclear war. Fortunately, reason and peace prevailed. This was the closest the superpowers came to directly battling each other in the forty-plus years of the Cold War, and it frightened the world.

Vietnam: Operation Phoenix

The Cold War became intensely heated again during the Vietnam War. When

A U.S. Army Ranger trains a Vietnamese soldier in 1962.

French colonial rule ended in 1954, Vietnam was divided into North Vietnam and South Vietnam. In the North, the Communist leader, Ho Chi Minh, served as president, and in the South, Ngo Dinh Diem ruled. Elections were scheduled to be held in 1956 to reunite all of Vietnam, but President Diem cancelled them ostensibly believing that the Communist leader, Ho Chi Minh, would win and reunite Vietnam under a Communist government. As a result of Diem's actions, a civil war between the Northern Communists and the South began and escalated. Fearing that South Vietnam would fall to the Communists, the United States sent in the CIA to spread anti-Communist propaganda, ferret out Communist supporters, and assist anti-Communist groups in the South. As it became increasingly clear that the CIA would not be enough to "save" South Vietnam from Ho Chi Minh's guerrilla fighters, called the Vietcong, the United States began sending troops.

During the Vietnam War, the most extensive paramilitary operation staged by the CIA, and the most controversial, was Operation Phoenix. The program began in 1968, and, put simply, its goal was to catch all the Vietcong in South Vietnam and either imprison or kill them. The CIA did not do this directly; they acted as advisers to the South Vietnamese police, and supported them. Operation Phoenix began to pile up results. In 1969 roughly 20,000 Vietcong were "neutralized," which means that they were either im-

A U.S. soldier (left) sets fire to a Vietnamese village during the Vietnam War.

prisoned or dead—6,187 of these people were killed. However, there is a great deal of controversy as to how many of them were actually Vietcong.

Whole villages of people thought to be sympathetic to the Vietcong were tortured and murdered without any evidence of actual involvement. The South Vietnamese police, who were notoriously corrupt, extorted money from people suspected of being associated with the Vietcong. "The worst abuse of the Phoenix program was the use of hearsay, even malicious gossip in a deliberate effort to suppress a segment of the population," writes John Prados.

"Often feuds, political maneuvers, even gangster-style 'protection' rackets, fueled tips to Phoenix operatives."[47] Or, as one CIA man put it more succinctly, "They assassinated a lot of the wrong damn people."[48] There were rumors that Phoenix was an assassination program and while no proof has ever established the claim, innocent people surely suffered terrible abuses as a result of the operation. The program forever tarnished the CIA.

As the military role of the CIA increased with programs such as Operation Phoenix, the question of whether it should be at the disposal of presidents to be used in a military capacity was called into question. As long as the general populace of the United States believed war was just and necessary to fight Communism around the world, presidents had a great deal of leeway to use the CIA in a military capacity. However, in the case of Vietnam, not all U.S. citizens agreed that any sort of military action should be taken. This resulted in protests at home that had an impact on the willingness of politicians to wage war abroad. The Vietnam War was not popular, and as the CIA's role in questionable programs came to light, neither was the CIA. Congress called for an investigation into the organization and its relationship with presidents. New procedures were established to give Congress more control over the CIA and, for the remainder of the Cold War, its spies were never again so obviously used as soldiers.

Keeping Countries Communist

While the Soviet Union played a role in Korea, the Bay of Pigs, and Vietnam, its military forces were not directly involved. There were, however, three countries in which the Soviets resorted to military means to ensure they remained Communist and loyal to Moscow—Hungary in 1956, Czechoslovakia in 1968, and Afghanistan in 1979. In each of these instances the KGB played a significant role in quashing rebellion in these Cold War hot spots. In order to achieve these ends, the agency used deception and force.

Yuri Andropov organized the ambush and execution of several key Hungarian officials in 1956.

The KGB was first called upon to halt revolution in Hungary. On October 23, 1956, when 250,000 people took to the streets of Budapest to call for free elections and support Imre Nagy as president, the uprising proved too large to be handled solely by the KGB, and the Red Army was called upon to assist. However, the resistance was still too great, and Nagy seized power and called for the removal of Soviet troops. Once Nagy was in power, it became abundantly clear he would not be loyal to wishes of the Soviet government in Moscow. Quickly, the KGB—led by Yuri Andropov—snapped into action. Andropov deceived the Nagy government, telling Nagy that the Soviets were willing to negotiate the withdrawal of their troops from Hungary. Under the guise of negotiating the terms, Andropov lured key government officials to a banquet. At this banquet, the Nagy government officials were ambushed and executed. Later, the KGB also lured Nagy from asylum in the Yugoslav embassy to his death by promising him that he could return safely to his home; instead he was captured and executed.

Letter from Krushchev

The following excerpt from a letter from Nikita Khrushchev to John F. Kennedy was part of the correspondence between the two countries during the Cuban Missile Crisis. It can be found at http://cwihp.si.edu.

> Having presented these conditions to us, Mr. President, you have thrown down the gauntlet. Who asked you to do this? By what right have you done this? Our ties with the Republic of Cuba, as well as our relations with other nations, regardless of their political system, concern only the two countries between which these relations exist . . . .
>
> You, Mr. President, are . . . issuing an ultimatum, and you are threatening that if we do not obey your orders, you will then use force. Think about what you are saying! And you want to persuade me to agree to this! What does it mean to agree to these demands? It would mean for us to conduct our relations with other countries not by reason, but by yielding to tyranny. You are not appealing to reason; you want to intimidate us. . . .
>
> The Soviet government considers the violation of the freedom of navigation in international waters and air space to constitute an act of aggression propelling humankind into the abyss of a world nuclear-missile war. Therefore, the Soviet government cannot instruct captains of Soviet ships bound for Cuba to observe orders of American naval forces blockading this island. Our instructions to Soviet sailors are to observe strictly the generally accepted standards of navigation in international waters and not retreat one step from them. And, if the American side violates these rights, it must be aware of the responsibility it will bear for this act. To be sure, we will not remain mere observers of pirate actions by American ships in the open sea. We will then be forced on our part to take those measures we deem necessary and sufficient to defend our rights. To this end we have all that is necessary.
>
> Respectfully, /s/ N. Khrushchev

An Uzbek woman covers her face as Soviet troops stand at attention near the Afghan–Soviet border in 1989.

The KGB's use of deception and force worked so well in the crushing of the Hungarian revolution that many of the same tactics were used in Czechoslovakia twelve years later to put a stop to the revolutionary reforms of the government led by Alexander Dubcek. One important new tactic employed by the KGB was the use of NOCs disguised as travelers, businesspeople, and students from Western nations. The KGB believed that Czechoslovakian revolutionaries would be more likely to speak to sympathetic Westerners about their plans for rebellion than their fellow citizens. It was the job of the NOCs to infiltrate revolutionary groups, identify members, and discredit them. In addition,

the NOCs were asked to plant evidence that later could be used to justify a Soviet invasion. Christopher Andrew and Vasili Mitrokhin describe one such "plant":

On July 19 *Pravda* [the Soviet state newspaper] reported the discovery of a "secret cache" of American weapons near the West German border, some conveniently contained in packages marked "Made in the USA," which had allegedly been smuggled into Czechoslovakia. . . . The Soviet authorities, it claimed, had also obtained a copy of an American "secret plan" to overthrow the Prague regime.[49]

The Soviets used this evidence that the KGB had manufactured as a reason for the invasion of Czechoslovakia by the Red Army and eventually succeeded in forcibly removing Dubcek from power.

Afghanistan

The third and final time the Soviets resorted to military means to keep a country Communist during the Cold War was in Afghanistan. The conflict began in September 1979 when Hafizullah Amin seized power in Afghanistan. Realizing that Amin would not necessarily remain loyal to Moscow, the Soviet government called upon the KGB to assassinate him. The KGB tried to assassinate Amin quietly by poisoning him. When this failed, they resorted to a massive paramilitary campaign in which KGB officers dressed as Afghani soldiers stormed the palace and killed Amin.

However, the assassination did not bring about a stable, Communist government in Afghanistan and, therefore, was just the beginning of Soviet military involvement. As rebellious and revolutionary forces mounted attacks to seize power in Afghanistan, over one hundred thousand Soviet troops were deployed to stop the rebellion and support a government loyal to Moscow. However, this was an impossible battle for the Red Army and the KGB. "Afghanistan [was] our Vietnam," one KGB general said. "We [were] bogged down in a war we [could] not win and [could] not abandon. It [was] ridiculous. A mess."[50]

Aside from the KGB's early role in the assassination of Amin, it was also called upon to install a regime friendly to Moscow and eliminate all those who would oppose it. In the KGB effort to eliminate the opposition, many Afghanis were brutally tortured. The following testimonial comes from an Afghani woman who was teaching in Kabul when she was called in for questioning:

> [She] dared to protest . . . that her Soviet interrogator "did not have the right to question an Afghan in Afghanistan. This angered them and they tied [her] hands and burned [her] lips with a cigarette." On instructions from the Soviet interrogator, [Afghani Security Agency] officers then beat her unconscious. When the teacher revived, she was buried up to her neck in the snow. In the days that followed, electrified needles were pressed into her body.[51]

As was the case with Vietnam, there were no winners in the war in Afghanistan. In 1988 the Soviet troops finally withdrew, but the country was devastated. It is difficult to imagine what would have become of countries such as Korea, Cuba, Vietnam, and Afghanistan if there had been no Cold War. As it stands, the superpowers used military means to intervene in each of these countries' domestic politics in hopes of furthering their own foreign policy objectives.

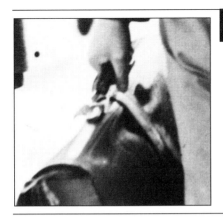

Chapter 7

Counter-intelligence

Spies do not steal just any information; they steal highly sensitive information. In fact, the whole point of espionage is to steal another nation's most carefully guarded secrets. The better protected the information is, the less likely it is that it will be stolen by an opposing intelligence agency, which is why nations take precautionary measures to guard their most valuable secrets. Collectively, these measures are called counterintelligence, or counterespionage. Throughout the Cold War, the KGB and the CIA used a variety of different tactics to protect their countries' secrets from each other's intelligence collection systems. They took security measures, placed individuals under surveillance, ran dangle operations, doubled agents, and utilized the information given them by defectors to catch spies.

Security and Surveillance

The simplest way to stop someone from stealing a secret is to lock it away in a place they cannot enter. Therefore, both the KGB and the CIA "lock away" information by protecting the buildings in which it is kept. At the outset of the Cold War, building security was very simplistic—guards, watchdogs, and electrified fences. However, as the Cold War progressed, both agencies began to utilize high-tech, effective security devices in an attempt to stop enemy agents from gaining access to certain buildings. Guards were replaced by security systems that required matching retinal scans to open doors. And watchdogs were replaced by state-of-the-art alarm systems that detected intruders by sound and heat as well as traditional methods. These sorts of systems made it significantly more difficult for hostile intelligence agencies even to gain access to buildings where important secrets were kept.

Once the building that held the information was more secure, it became important to control who had access to it.

Therefore, in the Cold War, intelligence agencies took precautions to ensure that the employees who came into contact with sensitive information were trustworthy. To accomplish this, the CIA and the KGB both initiated intensive screening processes for prospective officers. In the case of the CIA, this investigation involved any or all of the following: the potential employee's responses in an interview or on an application; a computerized check of all of the law enforcement and government databases; interviews with the person's friends, family, coworkers, and classmates (present and past); and at times, some sort of polygraph (lie-detector) test.

The KGB also relied heavily on the trustworthiness of its personnel. In *Inside the KGB* Aleksei Myagkov explains some of the security measures taken by the KGB when he entered its ranks. As a member of the Red Army, Myagkov decided he wanted to enter the KGB. He made this desire known to the chief of his section, Lieutenant Colonel Bloshchup, who preliminarily questioned him:

> Exactly a week [after Myagkov first indicated his interest to Bloshchup], I was sitting once more in the same room. This time it was the colonel who did most of the talking. He told me that during the week the KGB had

State-of-the-art security systems, such as this surveillance camera, continue to serve as an effective means of counterintelligence.

collected detailed testimonials and other references about me. All these were satisfactory, so that the probability of my being able to join up was not excluded, but this would become possible only after a careful vetting of me and my relatives. . . .

This took about three months, and during that time . . . my capabilities and qualities, the level of my general training and, of course, my knowledge of Marxism-Leninism, were tested. Besides that, I had to go before a strict medical commission.[52]

Having passed all these examinations, Myagkov was summoned to a final, brief interview and offered a position in the KGB. However, as Myagkov, who eventually defected from the KGB, is himself a testament to, even the most extensive personnel security measures cannot assure the loyalties of officers and agents.

Surveillance was another important component of the counterintelligence of both agencies during the Cold War. The basic idea was to identify agents and officers of hostile intelligence agencies and then watch their every move without them knowing it. Successful surveillance was made all the more difficult by the fact that the target's tradecraft had taught him or her complex tactics to evade surveillance. In addition, both agencies kept watch on their own officers. This was to make certain they were not compromised in any

way without their knowledge, and to make sure they were not betraying their agency.

Dangles

In the world of counterintelligence, a "dangle" is bait. Dangles are used to confuse, mislead, or infiltrate an intelligence agency. For example, if the KGB ran a dangle operation, it would select a trusted officer and construct an elaborate cover that made it appear as though he or she had access to information that the CIA wanted. They would also make it look as though the undercover officer was open to recruitment by the CIA. If the operation is successful, the CIA will recruit the person as an agent. The officer still reports back to the KGB, however, and now they have gained access to important CIA secrets. This would also expose the identity of the CIA officer, who might now be recruited, or "turned," to the KGB.

Another use of a dangle operation would be to have the dangled KGB officer feed the CIA useless or false information to mislead them while gaining insight into what they are seeking and why. The officer can also get a grasp on the methods used by the CIA to recruit individuals and the tradecraft they practice.

CIA officer David Atlee Phillips was the bait of a dangle operation in Chile early in his career. First, Phillips was given a cover as the chief of U.S. intelligence for Chile. Then, the KGB was allowed to "discover" that Phillips held this position (in reality, Phillips had only recently been recruited for the service and had no power). In his book *The Night Watch* Phillips explains what happened once he had been "dangled":

> I waited. Anyone who approached me was suspect: a stranger asking for directions on the street; a foreign diplomat being friendly at a cocktail party; an insistent insurance salesman. . . . What did a KGB agent look like? How did he act? . . .
>
> As I understood the rules of the mysterious game, there was no reason to tell [my case officer] of people with whom I became acquainted at my own initiative. I didn't tell her, for instance, of a new Chilean friend I was seeing fairly frequently.[53]

In reality, the KGB agent was Phillips's new Chilean friend, whom he did not suspect.

Since a dangle can collect a variety of information quite easily once the other agency takes the bait, as Harry Rositzke says, "The worst mistake any service can make is to recruit as an agent a man who has been 'dangled' before it by a hostile service."[54] Both the CIA and the KGB used dangle operations to gather information on each other during the Cold War.

Agents Provacateurs

The KGB took the concept of the dangle one step further during the Cold

Dangle operations were utilized by both superpowers during the Cold War.

War creating entire dangle organizations. The Soviets called their dangles *agents provacateurs,* and in the Cold War they used these agents to set up bogus anti-Communist organizations that the CIA then supported. In this way, the KGB tricked the CIA and the SIS into supplying them with money, arms, and technology.

One such deception operation took place in Poland in the early years of the Cold War. The anti-Communist Polish

Home Army (*Wolność I Niepodległość,* or WiN) was completely annihilated when the Soviets took control of the country. By 1947 the KGB had successfully eliminated any remaining members. Thus, WiN ceased to exist in 1947.

However, in 1948 the Polish secret police created a bogus WiN at the request of their KGB advisers. Shortly thereafter, they sent a "member" of the phony WiN group to London to tell the British that WiN was still in existence and in desperate need of financial and military support. The SIS and the CIA took the bait. Authors Christopher Andrew and Oleg Gordievsky explained the two intelligence agencies' reaction to this bogus organization:

Beginning in 1950, the CIA . . . began supplying the bogus WiN by parachute with arms, radio transmitters, and gold coins. . . . WiN demands for American assistance grew steadily. . . .

Then in December 1952 the [KGB] decided to expose the deception. A mocking two-hour broadcast on Polish radio revealed that a million dollars sent by the CIA to WiN over the past few years had ended up with Polish authorities.[55]

The WiN operation was one of a few known deceptions that the KGB staged during the Cold War. In each case, the CIA and/or the SIS was left looking very foolish for taking the bait of an entirely bogus rebel group or anti-Communist political organization. While the exposure of such hoaxes was certainly good propaganda for the Soviets, the operations had little counterintelligence value. They did deplete the CIA's resources and its confidence, but these elaborate fronts did little to expose CIA officers or plans.

Double Agents

Double agents were a staple of counterintelligence operations during the Cold War. A double agent is an officer who is discovered by the other service and then "turned," or converted, to work for them. Many double agents willingly switch loyalties for ideological, romantic, or monetary reasons. Selling out one's country for cash is not all that uncommon among intelligence officers. This led Soviet premier Khrushchev to tell the U.S. director of Central Intelligence, Allen Dulles, that the United States and the Soviet Union "could save money if they would stop paying the same spies."[56] There are even instances where agents, called triple or quadruple agents, have sold secrets to three or four intelligence agencies. Some double agents are not willing to sell information but have little or no choice; they are forced to provide information through blackmail and/or physical threats.

An intelligence agency may think they have "turned" an officer or agent when in reality that person has not changed allegiance. In this instance, an officer or agent pretends to be a double

Former CIA Director Allen Dulles sits in his Washington, D.C., office in 1954.

agent while feeding misinformation to the hostile agency or gathering information from it.

During the Cold War some intelligence agencies used double agents ambitiously and ingeniously. Abram Shulsky describes Cuba's suspected double agent "ring," which included not just one but many double agents. According to Shulsky, "an undetermined number of Cuban government officials, once believed by the United States to be secretly working for the CIA, were feeding the agency misleading or useless information prepared by the Cuban DGI (Cuba's Secret Service)."[57] While it is not clear how much important information these agents were able to obtain, the operation successfully wasted a great deal of CIA time, energy, and money. As an added bonus for the DGI, the spy ring's exposure in the press was an embarrassment to the CIA.

Defectors or Walk-ins

While double agents are discovered by the opposing agency and turned, defectors and walk-ins voluntarily contact the opposing intelligence service. During the Cold War the closed nature of Soviet society caused the United States to rely heavily on defectors and walk-ins in its counterintelligence efforts. Since it was nearly impossible to spot and recruit a KGB officer to work for the CIA, counterintelligence officers had to wait for KGB officers to come to them. The Soviets also relied on walk-ins, but not to the same extent as the CIA.

One of the most infamous KGB defectors was code clerk Igor Gouzenko. Gouzenko's information led to some of the most well-known counterespionage arrests in U.S. history. It was Gouzenko's information that helped the authorities catch atomic spy Klaus Fuchs, who received a fourteen-year sentence after pleading guilty in 1951. Gouzenko's codebooks and ciphering knowledge were of

A Double Agent Explains Why

One of the most infamous double agents in CIA history was Aldrich Ames. In 1985, toward the end of the Cold War, Ames, a CIA agent, began selling information to the Soviets. This information led to the arrest and execution of ten CIA agents. Ames was interviewed for CNN's Cold War series and discussed why he sold U.S. secrets to the Soviets. An excerpt of this interview is printed below as it was found at www.cnn.com.

At the time that I handed over the names and compromised so many CIA agents in the Soviet Union . . . I had come to the conclusion that the loss of these sources to the United States government, or to the West as well, would not compromise significant national defense, political, [or] diplomatic interests. . . . And I would say that this belief of the noninjurious nature of what I was doing . . . permitted me to do what I did for much more personal reasons. . . .

The reasons that I did what I did in April of 1985 were personal, banal, and amounted really to a kind of greed and folly. As simple as that. [I decided] to do that in order to make some quick and easy money, at very low risk and doing very little damage. Because at that time, in April, I saw [my actions] as almost like a scam I was running on the KGB: by giving them people that I knew were their double agents. . . .

It was a matter of pursuing an intensely personal agenda, of trying to make some money that I felt I needed very badly, and in a sense that I felt at the time, one of terrible desperation. I mean, you might as well ask why a middle-aged man with no criminal record might go and put a paper bag over his head and rob a bank. I mean, it's that kind of dramatic, and perhaps interesting, but when you get right down to it, kind of banal answer.

great use in the VENONA decrypts, which then led the FBI to David Greenglass and Julius and Ethel Rosenberg.

The information that Gouzenko gave the CIA was remarkable, and he was just one in a long line of defectors that the CIA used to ferret out KGB spies in the United States. However, the KGB also sent a great many fake defectors to the CIA, people who fed them misinformation as to Soviet intentions. As a result, the CIA had to be very careful when interrogating potential defectors to make sure they were legitimate.

Precautions, CI-Nicks, and Assassinations

In order to limit the amount of harm the defection of one agent or officer to the other side can cause, intelligence agencies take certain precautions against double agents, defectors, and walk-ins. These include limiting the information available to them, spying on them and even assassinating them.

Since a good deal of the damage caused by double agents is their ability to identify other agents for the hostile service, intelligence agents and officers know the real names, appearance, and duties of a very limited number of their coworkers. This is especially true during training when new personnel are involved and their trustworthiness has not yet been proven. "There were other agents in the safe house, but I never saw them," David Atlee Phillips recalls about

his training facility. "When I went to the john my instructor would check first to be sure it was not occupied by another student."[58]

Author Harry Rositzke explains just how little the average KGB officer knows about his or her fellow comrades:

> For many KGB agents where live meetings are essential, his case officer is a man without a real name . . . without an address, with an unknown job or office. Where the operation simply requires the passage of reports or documents

David Greenglass leaves the New York House of Detention in 1960.

one way, and money and instructions the other, the agent knows only the dead drops . . . he is instructed to use. He does not know where his documents go. . . . He does not know who his real boss is—nor, in many cases, even whether he is working for the KGB.[59]

In addition to limiting the amount of information about their coworkers that intelligence officers can access, the CIA and the KGB also employ officers who specialize in counterespionage. In the case of the CIA, they are positioned at nearly every station around the globe. These counterintelligence officers, or CI-Nicks as other officers call them, monitor all the espionage and covert action operations of the station. Throughout the Cold War (and still today) these CI-Nicks looked over all of the agents' and officers' reports for any sign of penetration by hostile intelligence agencies. They set up dangle operations, turned KGB agents for use as doubles, and kept surveillance on any CIA officers they felt might turn to the KGB. Since it is the CI-Nick's job to suspect everyone and see treachery everywhere, they have earned a special reputation in the agency. "In an agency full of

extremely mistrustful people, they are the professional paranoids,"[60] write Marchetti and Marks.

While the KGB was dedicated to catching any traitors in its midst, they took counterintelligence to a whole new level. Once they identified a defector or a double agent, they were intent on shutting down the leak and punishing the traitor so as to deter further defections. The following excerpt from a document of Mitrokhin's archive illustrates the KGB's stance on the issue:

The KGB must intensify the spirit of hatred towards the enemy and traitors. Significant harm is done by the comforting theory that losses are inevitable in wars between intelligence services

The Gouzenko Transcripts

In *The Gouzenko Transcripts: The Evidence Presented to the Kellock-Taschereau Royal Commission of 1946*, Gouzenko describes some of the security measures undertaken by the KGB to safeguard its codes and highly protected transmissions. In this passage, Gouzenko is being questioned by E.K. Williams:

GOUZENKO: The code books were kept in a sealed bag, which I handed to the chief of the division, Aleksashkin. . . .

The procedure is as follows. I would ring the secret bell and a little aperture in the steel door would be opened and Aleksashkin would look through. I would ask him if there were any telegrams, and if there were any telegrams I would get

[from] him the sealed sack with the code and the telegrams. If Colonel Zabotin wished to send some telegrams to Moscow, I would ask him for the bag, the sealed sack. . . .

WILLIAMS: And when you had finished your coding, what would you do with the code?

GOUZENKO: I placed the code back in the sack and sealed it with my seal and took the sack back to Aleksashkin.

WILLIAMS: And what would you do with the originals of the telegrams or other communications that you had coded?

GOUZENKO: The originals were placed in a file and the file, along with the code, was placed in the pouch, the sealed pouch.

. . . betrayals are sometimes called compromises. Compromises, by which is meant operational failures, are usually provoked by skillful dangles by the enemy. Equating these two concepts usually leads to the moral justification of traitors, and creates an image of them as victims of the intelligence skills of the enemy. Defectors do not go unpunished. Their punishment is described in such proverbs as: . . . "A traitor is his own murderer."[61]

Their solution was to assassinate the defector. At the top of their most-wanted list sat men such as Gouzenko. Unfortunately for the KGB, it usually proved too difficult to locate the defector, which is not surprising since they had been given top-notch KGB training in the tradecraft of espionage.

Counterespionage tactics such as the assassination of defectors, state-of-the-art security systems, surveillance, double agents, and dangles, were employed by the KGB and the CIA in an effort to stop hostile intelligence agencies from gathering information throughout the Cold War. Whereas electrified fences and watchdogs were viewed as sufficient at the start of the Cold War, forty years later both agencies had learned that these measures were not enough to stop capable spies. As technology developed—and along with it the need to protect new technologies—the superpowers found both new ways to spy on each other and new ways to safeguard their secrets. By the end of the Cold War, thwarting the other superpower's attempt to gather information was just as important as collecting information.

☆ Epilogue ☆

The Post–Cold War World

Hungary, Poland, Lithuania, Estonia, and Latvia had already declared their sovereignty from the Soviet Union as thousands of East Germans gathered in front of the Berlin Wall on November 9, 1989. For twenty-eight years, the Wall had served as a constant visual reminder of the Cold War. Standing in front of the Wall that day, the East Germans chanted, *Wir sind das Volk* (We are the people). No guards fired upon them; no troops were called out as they had been in 1953. The people continued chanting until the borders opened, the Wall "came down," Berlin was united again, and East Germany declared its sovereignty. Soon after, Czechoslovakia declared its independence from the Soviet Union.

This, then, marked the end of the Cold War. The United States claimed victory and, with the dissolution of the Soviet Union, took its seat at the head of the table as the world's only superpower.

People pass freely through the once heavily guarded Berlin Wall in 2001.

With the Cold War's end, both the United States and the countries that made up the former USSR looked out on a new world with new challenges.

For the CIA and the KGB this marked the end of an era in which espionage and technical intelligence collection had come of age. Incredible new technologies and tragic world events had altered the role of the intelligence officer in both organizations. While the start of the Cold War had seen KGB spies snooping around and infiltrating the Manhattan Project to steal top-secret atomic information, the end of the Cold War showed spies training paramilitary troops in times of presumed peace and fighting secret wars.

In the post–Cold War world, the role of the spy continues to evolve as new types of adversaries present themselves. While the "bad guys" were obvious throughout the Cold War, after 1989 it has become more difficult to figure out who is a threat and why. Terrorist groups around the world and other nations that have successfully developed nuclear weapons pose a very different threat to Russia and the United States, who now work together against some of these parties. Their intelligence agencies fight every day to adapt to the new world in which they operate.

☆ Notes ☆

Introduction: The Importance of Espionage in the Cold War

1. Quoted in Martin Walker, *The Cold War: A History*. New York: Henry Holt and Company, 1993, p. 12.

2. Quoted in Walker, *The Cold War*, p. 40.

Chapter 1: Officers and Agents

3. Harry Rositzke, *The KGB: The Eyes of Russia*. Garden City, NY: Doubleday & Company, 1981, pp. 235–36.

4. David W. Doyle, *True Men and Traitors: From the OSS to the CIA, My Life in the Shadows*. New York: John Wiley & Sons, 2001, p. 102.

5. Quoted in Christopher Andrew and Vasili Mitrokhin, *The Sword and the Shield: The Mitrokhin Archive and the Secret History of the KGB*. New York: Basic Books, 1999, p. 58.

6. Abram N. Shulsky, *Silent Warfare: Understanding the World of Intelligence*. Washington, DC: Brassey's, 1993, p. 12.

7. Former Defense Intelligence Agency case officer, interview with author, January 25, 2002.

8. Former Defense Intelligence Agency case officer, interview with author, January 25, 2002.

9. Aleksei Myagkov, *Inside the KGB: An Expose by an Officer of the Third Directorate*. London: Foreign Affairs, 1976, pp. 70–71.

10. Myagkov, *Inside the KGB*, p. 45.

11. David Atlee Phillips, *The Night Watch*. New York: Atheneum, 1977, p. 12.

12. Shulsky, *Silent Warfare*, p. 21.

13. National Security Agency (www.nsa. gov).

14. Victor Marchetti and John D. Marks, *The CIA and the Cult of Intelligence*. New York: Alfred A. Knopf, 1974, p. 266.

15. Former Defense Intelligence Agency case officer, interview with author, January 25, 2002.

16. Former Defense Intelligence Agency case officer, interview with author, January 25, 2002.

Chapter 2: Cloak-and-Dagger Work in the Cold War

17. Christopher Andrew and Oleg Gordievsky, *KGB: The Inside Story*. New York: HarperPerennial, 1991, p. 376.

18. Andrew and Gordievsky, *KGB*, pp. 316–17.

19. Andrew and Gordievsky, *KGB*, p. 316.

20. Andrew and Gordievsky, *KGB*, p. 216.

21. Richard Aldrich, ed., *Espionage, Security and Intelligence in Britain 1945–1970.* Manchester, UK: Manchester University Press, 1998, p. 140.

22. Quoted in Andrew and Mitrokhin, *The Sword and the Shield*, p. 205.

23. Andrew and Gordievsky, *KGB*, p. 526.

24. Quoted in Andrew and Mitrokhin, *The Sword and the Shield*, p. 137.

25. Quoted in Nathan Miller, *Spying for America: The Hidden History of U.S. Intelligence.* New York: Marlowe & Company, 1997, p. 346.

26. Quoted in Miller, *Spying for America*, p. 346.

Chapter 3: Technology and the Changing Role of the Spy

27. Marchetti and Marks, *The CIA and the Cult of Intelligence*, p. 188.

28. Shulsky, *Silent Warfare*, pp. 24–25.

29. Ernest Volkman and Blaine Baggett, *Secret Intelligence.* New York: Doubleday, 1989, p. 187.

30. Paul Hoversten, "CORONA: Celebrating 40 Years of Spy Satellites," Space-News. www.space.com.

31. Volkman and Baggett, *Secret Intelligence*, p. 191.

Chapter 4: Listening In: Communications Intelligence During the Cold War

32. Volkman and Baggett, *Secret Intelligence*, pp. 59–60.

33. Volkman and Baggett, *Secret Intelligence*, p. 60.

34. *Cold War International History Project*, "KGB 1967 Annual Reports." http://cwihp.si.edu.

35. Andrew and Mitrokhin, *The Sword and the Shield*, p. 344.

36. Miller, *Spying for America*, p. 326.

37. Andrew and Mitrokhin, *The Sword and the Shield*, p. 400.

Chapter 5: Active Measures and Covert Operations

38. Quoted in Shulsky, *Silent Warfare*, p. 85.

39. Andrew and Gordievsky, *KGB*, p. 344.

40. Miller, *Spying for America*, p. 359.

41. Andrew and Mitrokhin, *The Sword and the Shield*, pp. 356–57.

42. Phillips, *The Night Watch*, p. 42.

Chapter 6: The Cold War Heats Up

43. Quoted in Andrew aud Gordievsky, *KGB*, p. 394.

44. Quoted in Miller, *Spying for America*, p. 321.

45. Marchetti and Marks, *The CIA and the Cult of Intelligence*, p. 309.

46. Miller, *Spying for America*, p. 368.

47. John Prados, *Presidents' Secret Wars: CIA and Pentagon Covert Operations Since World War II.* New York: William Morrow and Company, p. 310.

48. Quoted in Miller, *Spying for America*, p. 379.

49. Andrew and Mitrokhin, *The Sword and the Shield*, p. 255.

50. Quoted in Andrew and Gordievsky, *KGB*, p. 576.

51. Quoted in Andrew and Gordievsky, *KGB*, p. 577.

Chapter 7: Counterintelligence

52. Myagkov, *Inside the KGB*, p. 18.

53. Phillips, *The Night Watch*, p. 16.

54. Rositzke, *The KGB: The Eyes of Russia*, p. 237.

55. Andrew and Gordievsky, *KGB*, p. 388.

56. Phillips, *The Night Watch*, p. 205.

57. Shulsky, *Silent Warfare*, pp. 128–29.

58. Phillips, *The Night Watch*, p. 12.

59. Rositzke, *The KGB: The Eyes of Russia*, pp. 239–40.

60. Marchetti and Marks, *The CIA and the Cult of Intelligence*, p. 213.

61. Quoted in Andrew and Mitrokhin, *The Sword and the Shield*, pp. 366–67.

★ For Further Reading ★

Books

John Barron, *KGB: The Secret Work of Secret Agents.* New York: Reader's Digest Press, 1974. Despite its age, this is a fairly accessible book. While it only includes history of the KGB through the early 1970s, it also has some interesting documents available in its appendixes.

Fitzroy Maclean, *Take Nine Spies.* London: Weidenfeld and Nicolson, 1978. This book contains short biographies of nine real-life spies.

David Atlee Phillips, *The Night Watch.* New York: Atheneum, 1977. David Atlee Phillips was a very influential CIA officer in his time. His autobiography is very readable and lets the reader see into the life of an officer.

Websites

CNN's Cold War Series (www.cnn.com).

Cold War International History Project (www.cwihp.si.edu).

Cold War Museum (www.coldwar.org). This site gives a good general history, has trivia games, and an excellent link to a resources section.

US Historical Documents Archive (http://w3.one.net).

Internet Services

National Security Agency VENONA decryption. www.nsa.gov.

⋆ Works Consulted ⋆

Books

Richard Aldrich, ed., *Espionage, Security and Intelligence in Britain 1945–1970*. Manchester, UK: Manchester University Press, 1998. Contains primary documents on espionage in Britain during the Cold War. Because of the close alliance between U.S. and UK intelligence agencies, it does have some documents that deal with CIA and KGB issues.

Christopher Andrew and Oleg Gordievsky, *KGB: The Inside Story*. New York: Harper-Perennial, 1991. This book is somewhat difficult, but a good read. It provides an excellent in-depth look at the KGB and its activities during the Cold War.

Christopher Andrew and Vasili Mitrokhin, *The Sword and the Shield: The Mitrokhin Archive and the Secret History of the KGB*. New York: Basic Books, 1999. One of the most insightful books written on the KGB to date. It is filled with thousands of interesting facts about the KGB and its operations throughout the Cold War. It is a wonderful book for an advanced reader.

Robert Bothwell and J.L. Granstein, ed., *The Gouzenko Transcripts: The Evidence Presented to the Kellock-Taschereau Royal Commission of 1946*. Deneau Publishers & Company, 1946. The name says it all. This is a transcript of Gouzenko's questioning by the Canadian authorities after his defection.

Dr. Ray S. Cline, *The CIA Under Reagan, Bush, and Casey: The Evolution of the Agency from Roosevelt to Reagan*. Washington, DC: Acropolis Books Ltd., 1981. Cline is a former deputy director of the CIA and in this book he sets out to tell its history. There are some interesting anecdotes.

David W. Doyle, *True Men and Traitors: From the OSS to the CIA, My Life in the Shadows*. New York: John Wiley & Sons, 2001. This is an interesting autobiography of Doyle's life as a spy. Since Doyle was stationed in Africa, it lends insight into U.S. intelligence operations there.

Victor Marchetti and John D. Marks, *The CIA and the Cult of Intelligence*. New York: Alfred A. Knopf, 1974. This is a good overview of the CIA written in the midst of the Cold War. However, it is difficult to read due to deleted passages (perhaps censored by the CIA/FBI).

Nathan Miller, *Spying for America: The Hidden History of U.S. Intelligence*. New York: Marlowe, 1997. This is a very interesting, readable overview of U.S. intelligence from the American Revolution through the early 1990s.

Aleksei Myagkov, *Inside the KGB: An Exposé by an Officer of the Third Directorate.* London: Foreign Affairs, 1976. This is a very easy read and provides a firsthand account of life in the KGB as well as how the author defected from the service.

John Prados, *Presidents' Secret Wars: CIA and Pentagon Covert Operations Since World War II.* New York: William Morrow, 1986. Prados's book deals with the evolution of presidents' use of the CIA to wage secret wars.

Harry Rositzke, *The KGB: The Eyes of Russia.* Garden City, NY: Doubleday, 1981. This is a very accessible book about the KGB in which chapters revolve around a variety of issues from the use of the KGB in Stalin's Terror to assassins and counterespionage.

Jerrold L. Schecter and Peter S. Deriabin, *The Spy Who Saved the World: How a Soviet Colonel Changed the Course of the Cold War.* New York: Charles Scribner's Sons. This is the story of Colonel Penkovsky, a Soviet intelligence officer who worked as a double agent supplying the West with information until he was caught, tried, and shot by the KGB.

Abram N. Shulsky, *Silent Warfare: Understanding the World of Intelligence.* Washington, DC: Brassey's, 1993, Shulsky takes a political science approach to intelligence, defining, fleshing out, and describing all its components. He also includes some interesting examples of each aspect of intelligence. A great book for advanced readers.

Pavel and Anatoli Sudoplatov, *Special Tasks: The Memoirs of an Unwanted Witness—a Soviet Spymaster.* Boston: Little, Brown, 1995. This is a great story, but it focuses mostly on the years preceding the Cold War in the Soviet Union. However, there is a good bit about the Soviet atomic spy ring.

Ernest Volkman and Blaine Baggett, *Secret Intelligence.* New York: Doubleday, 1989. This is a good, easy, and entertaining overview of the CIA's activities during the Cold War.

Martin Walker, *The Cold War: A History.* New York: Henry Holt, 1993. Walker's book provides a good overview of the basic events of the Cold War in a straightforward manner. Not too difficult for young readers.

Periodicals

Christopher Andrew, "Intelligence and International Relations in the Early Cold War," *Review of International Studies,* July 1998.

Desmond Ball and Robert Windrem, "Soviet Signals Intelligence (Sigint): Organization and Management," *Intelligence and National Security,* October 1989.

Anthony Blunt, "From Bloomsbury to Marxism," *Studio International,* November 1973.

Newsweek, "Germany: 'I Have Come to Kill,'" May 3, 1954.

William Rosenau, "A Deafening Silence:

US Policy and the Sigint Facility at Lourdes," *Intelligence and National Security,* October 1994.

Time, "THE NATION," May 16, 1960.

Internet Sources

Cold War International History Project, "KGB 1967 Annual Report." http://cwihp.si.edu.

Paul Hoversten, "CORONA: Celebrating 40 Years of Spy Satellites," *SpaceNews.* www.space.com.

Websites

CIA (www.cia.gov).

National Security Agency (www.nsa.gov).

Spy Tech Agency Online Catalog (http://store.yahoo.com).

✷ Index ✷

active measures, 60–61

aerial reconnaissance, 25, 42–45

see also satellite spying

Afghanistan, 68–69, 81, 83, 84

agents, 15–16, 26–27

agents provacateurs (counterintelligence agents), 88–89

Air Force Intelligence, 12

see also Central Intelligence Agency

Ames, Aldrich, 91

Amin, Hafizullah, 68–69

Andrew, Christopher, 32, 34, 35, 62, 67, 89

Andropov, Yuri, 68–69, 81, 82

Arbenz, Jacobo, 69

Armas, Carlos Castillo, 69

Army Intelligence, 12

see also Central Intelligence Agency

assassinations, 67–69

atomic bomb, 8, 11, 28–32, 42

Baggett, Blaine, 45

Barron, John, 26

Bay of Pigs invasion, 75–77

Berlin, 56–59

Berlin Wall, 95

Big Three, 8

Bissell, Richard M., 45, 46

blackmail, 20–21, 26

Blake, George, 35, 58, 59

Blunt, Anthony, 33–35

Bond, James, 14–15

bribery, 26, 65

British Secret Service, 33–35

see also Secret Intelligence Service

British Security Service (MI5), 33

Broz, Josip. *See* Tito, Marshall

brush pass, 23

buffer zone, 8, 61–62

"bugs" (hidden listening devices), 49–51

Bulgaria, 64

Burgess, Guy, 33–35

Cairncross, John, 33–35

Cambridge Ring, 33–35

Camp Peary, 22

Camp Trax, 76–77

capitalism, 9

case officer (CO), 20

Castro, Fidel, 68, 75, 77

Cecil, Robert, 73

Central Intelligence Agency (CIA)

anti-Communist organizations and, 88

Chile and, 87–88

Congress and, 81

counterespionage and, 87–94

Cuba and, 75–77, 90

functions of, 12–13

gadgets of, 40–41

Guatemala and, 69–70, 75–77

Korea and, 73–74

recruiting, 16, 18–22
training for, 22–24,
91–92
wire tapping and,
56–59
Chile, 87–88
China, 74
*CIA, Under Reagan,
Bush & Casey, The: The
Evolution of the Agency
from Roosevelt to Reagan*
(Cline), 64
CI-Nicks, 93–94
ciphers. *See* codes
Cline, Ray S., 64
cloak-and-dagger work,
28
code breaking. *See*
codes
codes, 51–55
Cold War, 10–12
communications
intelligence
(COMINT), 74
communism, 9
computer science, 24
concealment. *See*
cover
Congo, 67
Contras, 67
controller, 20
CORONA (spy

satellite), 46–47
counterespionage,
85–94
countersurveillance, 24
cover, 17–19
covert action agents, 15
covert operations, 60
cryptanalysis, 24, 51–55
cryptology, 74
Cuba, 75–79, 90
Cuban Missile Crisis,
76–79, 82
Czechoslovakia, 64–65,
81, 95

dangles, 87–88
dead drops, 21, 23
decoding. *See* codes;
cryptanalysis
decrypting, 43–44
see also codes;
cryptanalysis
defectors, 37–38, 90–91
Defense Intelligence
Agency (DIA), 12, 27
Deriabin, Peter S., 21
Deutch, Arnold, 16–17,
33
Directorate of Science
and Technology,
40–41
Director of Central

Intelligence (DCI), 48
Discoverer. See CORONA
double agents, 15,
89–90
see also counter-
espionage
Doyle, David W., 15
Dubcek, Alexander,
83–84
Dulles, Allen, 89

Eastern Europe, 64–65,
95
East Germany, 55, 64,
95
elections, 64–65, 69–70
engineering, 15
espionage, 14–15, 85
executive actions,
67–69

false-flag recruitments,
16
Federal Bureau of
Investigation (FBI),
23
financial aid, 65
First Chief Directorate
(FCD), 12, 40
foreign policy, 60
*From Bloomsbury to
Marxism* (Blunt), 34

Fuchs, Klaus, 30–31, 37, 90

gadgets, 25
  see also "bugs"
Gardner, Meredith, 54
Germany, 95
Gomulka, Wladyslaw, 62–63
Gordievsky, Oleg, 89
Gottlieb, Stanley, 67
Gouzenko, Igor, 37, 54, 90–91, 93
Gouzenko Transcripts, The: Evidence Presented to the Kellock-Taschereau Royal Commission of 1946 (Gouzenko), 93
Greenglass, David, 31, 91
GRU (Soviet military intelligence), 37
Guatemala, 69–70
guerrilla fighters, 80

Ho Chi Minh, 80
Home Army (Poland), 62–63
Hood, William, 37
human intelligence (HUMINT), 14–16, 35, 47–48

Hungary, 64, 81
HVA (East German foreign intelligence department), 55

infiltration, 87–88
Inside the KGB: An Expose by an Officer of the Third Directorate (Myagkov), 18, 20, 22, 86–87
intelligence agencies, 12
  See also names of specific agencies
intelligence analysis, 24
Iraq, 67–68
Irish Republican Army (IRA), 66
Israel, 38, 66
Italy, 64–65

Johnson, Clarence L. "Kelly," 45
Joint Chiefs of Staff (JCS), 34–35

Kassem, Abdul Karim, 67–68
Kennan, George F., 10
Kennedy, John F., 76, 77, 79, 82

KGB
  Afghanistan and, 84
  Bay of Pigs invasion and, 81
  British agencies and, 33–35
  Cuba and, 75
  Czechoslovakia and, 81, 83–84
  functions of, 12–13
  history of, 12, 28
  Hungary and, 81, 82–83
  Korea and, 72–73, 81
  phone line scrambling and, 57
  Poland and, 62–64
  police duty and, 22–23
  recruiting for, 16–17, 18–22, 26, 33
  training for, 22–24
  Vietnam and, 81
  Walker family and, 35–36
KGB: The Inside Story (Andrew), 34
KGB: The Secret Work of Secret Agents (Barron), 26
Kim Il-Sung, 71–73
Korea, 71–74

Kruschev, Nikita, 37–38, 44, 79, 82, 89

Land, Edwin, 45
leaks, 93–94
Lebanon, 51
Leghorn, Richard, 46
Lenin, Vladimir Ilyich, 9
Lockheed Aircraft, 45
Los Alamos, 31
Lumumba, Patrice, 67

Maclean, Donald, 31, 33–35, 72
Mafia, 68
Magnificent Five, 33–35, 72
Manhattan Project, 28–32, 96
Marchetti, Victor, 26–27, 40–41, 78, 93
Marks, John D., 26–27, 40–41, 78, 93
Marx, Karl, 9
May, Allan Nunn, 32, 37
MI5. *See* British Security Service
MIGs (Russian fighter jets), 43, 78
Miller, Nathan, 37, 57, 67–68

Mitrokhin, Vasili, 55, 58, 67, 83–84, 93–94
moles, 15, 59
Mossad (Israeli intelligence agency), 38
Myagkov, Aleksei, 18, 20, 22, 86–87

Nagy, Imre, 82
National Security Agency (NSA), 12, 24, 45
Navy Intelligence, 12
see also Central Intelligence Agency
Nelson, Carl, 7
Ngo Diem Dinh, 80
Nicaragua, 66–67
Night Watch, The (Phillips), 23, 76, 87
non-official cover officers (NOCs), 18–19, 25–26
North Korea. *See* Korea
North Vietnam. *See* Vietnam
nuclear weapons. *See* atomic bomb

Operation Candy, 37
Operation Gold, 55–59

Operation of Policy Coordination (OPC), 74–75
Operation Phoenix, 80–81
Operation Pluto, 75–77
Operation Stole, 73–74

Palestine, 38
paramilitary, 60, 74, 76–77, 80
see also Cuba; Korea
payments, 26–27
Peierls, Rudolf, 31
Penkovsky, Oleg Vladimirovich, 39
Philby, Kim, 33–35, 72
Phillips, David Atlee, 23, 69–70, 87–88, 91–92
photo reconnaissance. *See* aerial reconnaissance; satellite spying
piston agents, 15–16
POCHIN (Soviet radio intercepting device), 54–55
"pocket litter," 19
poisoning, 67–68
Poland, 62–64, 88–89
Popov, Pyotr

Semyonovich, 37

Popular Front for the Liberation of Palestine, 66

Powers, Francis Gary, 44, 46

Prados, John, 80–81

Pravda (newspaper), 83–84

PROBA (Soviet radio intercepting device), 54–55

propaganda, 60, 61, 69–70, 75, 80

proxies. *See* terrorist groups

radio stations, 69–70, 75

radio transmission, 51–55

RB-47, 42–45

Roosevelt, Franklin D., 8

Rosenberg, Ethel, 31, 91

Rosenberg Julius, 31, 91

Rositzke, Harry, 87–88, 92–93

Rumania, 64

sabotage, 60

safe house, 23, 91–92

Samos 2 (spy satellite), 46–47

SAMs (surface-to-air missiles), 43–45, 78

Sandinista Liberation Front, 66–67

satellite spying, 45–47

satellite states, 8

Schecter, Jerold L., 21

Secret Intelligence Service (SIS), 33–35, 51, 57, 88–89

security, 85–87

Shulsky, Abram, 17, 24, 44, 90

signals analysis, 24

Silent Warfare (Shulsky), 17

sleeper agents, 15–16

South Korea. *See* Korea

South Vietnam. *See* Vietnam

Special Tasks: The Memoirs of an Unwanted Witness —a Soviet Spymaster (Sudoplatov and Sudoplatov), 32

spies. *See* agents

spy satellites, 25
  see also, CORONA

Spy Who Saved the World, The: How a Soviet Colonel Changed the Course of the Cold War (Schecter and Deriabin), 21

Stalin, Joseph, 29–30, 61–64

Stasi (East German state police), 55

Sudoplatov, Anatoli, 32

Sudoplatov, Pavel, 32

surface-to-air-missiles. *See* SAMs

surveillance, 23, 87

Sword and Shield, The: The Mitrokhin Archive and the Secret History of the KGB (Andrew and Mitrokhin), 67

technical intelligence, 24–25

Technical Services Division (TSD), 40

technology, 24–25, 40–41, 95
  see also "bugs"; gadgets; surveillance

telephone conversations, 55–59

terrorist groups, 65–67

Tito, Marshall, 67, 68

tradecraft, 23–24

triple agents, 15
Truman, Harry S., 32, 65, 72
tunnel, 57, 58–59
Turner, Stansfield, 48

U-2 (spy plane), 45–47, 48, 78–79

Vatican, 65
VENONA (Soviet code), 53–54, 56, 91

Vietcong, 80
Vietnam, 79–81
Vladivostock, 73, 74
Voice of Liberation, 69–70
Volkman, Ernest, 45, 48, 52–53, 54

Walker, Arthur, 35
Walker, John, 35–36
Walker, Michael, 35
walk-ins, 35, 37–38, 90–91
watchers, 42
Whitworth, Jerry, 35
wiretapping, 55–59
Wolf, Markus, 55
World War II, 6, 8, 42, 56

yavkas (KGB agent meeting places), 38
Yongdo Island, 74
Yugoslavia, 67, 68

★ About the Author ★

Jennifer Keeley is a freelance writer and former teacher who lives and works in Seattle, Washington. She graduated from Carleton College in 1996 with a degree in history and her teaching certificate. She has taught history and social studies in both the Seattle and Minneapolis public schools.